How to Write
Successful Magazine Articles

✵

CAMILLE DAVIED ROSE

Boston

THE WRITER, INC.

Publishers

ACKNOWLEDGMENTS

In my class meetings with students in non-fiction writing whose discussions I was privileged to lead in the School of Continuing Education at New York University, I proceeded from the conviction that one good example was worth two hours of lecture. As each topic came up for examination, I assigned for reading an illustrative article or quotation from some periodical or book which was on the newsstands or in the book stores at the time.

Since I cannot foresee what pertinent articles will be current for the readers of this book, I have made selections of excerpts and entire articles which seem to me to provide solutions to many of the problems new writers will meet. I am, therefore, especially grateful to the following publishers and writers for their permission to reprint various selections:

To *Coronet Magazine,* and the authors of the following: "Reading Writing" by Theodore Irwin, Copyright © 1966 by H. S. Publications, Inc. Excerpts from "The Tiniest Tycoon" by Dixie Dean Trainor, Copyright © 1964 by H. S. Publications, Inc., and "Diets," Copyright © 1965 by H. S. Publications, Inc.

To *Good Housekeeping,* and the authors of the following: excerpt from "Some of the Nicest People Are Superstitious" by Winifred Wolfe; excerpt from "Must These Children Live Without Love?" by Arlene Silberman (also to Mrs. Silberman for permission to include one of her early versions of the lead to this article).

To Harcourt, Brace & World, Inc., for the opening paragraph of *Elmer Gantry* by Sinclair Lewis.

To Harper & Row, for the excerpt from page 118, "Will Strunk" in *The Points of My Compass* by E. B. White (Harper & Row, 1962). And to the Macmillan Company for the same excerpt from the Introduction to *The Elements of Style* by Strunk and White, Copyright © 1959 by The Macmillan Company.

To *Look,* for the following: excerpt from "The Audacious World of Adam Powell" by Ernest Dunbar; excerpt from "Dating by Computer" produced by Gene Shalit.

To *McCall's Magazine,* for the following: excerpt from "Five Came to Aberdeen" by Alice Lake; excerpt from "Meet the Queen of Greece" by Camille Davied.

To *The New York Times Magazine,* and the author for "We Ask the Wrong Questions About Crime" by William M. McCord. Copyright © 1965 by The New York Times Company. Reprinted by permission.

To *The Reader's Digest* and the authors of the following: "You're Smarter Than You Think" by John Kord Lagemann. Copyright © 1953 by The Reader's Digest Association, Inc. (Mr. Lagemann's notes on "How I Wrote It" appeared in *A Guide to Successful Magazine Writing.*) "The Most Unforgettable Character I've Met," by Sam Shumate. Copyright © 1962 by The Reader's Digest Association, Inc. "Cholesterol: Guilty or Not Guilty?" by J. D. Ratcliff. Copyright © 1964 by The Reader's Digest Association, Inc. "Boyhood on the Prairie" by Ben Hibbs. Copyright © 1964 by The Reader's Digest Association, Inc. Excerpt from "My Most Unforgettable Character" by Jean Libman Block. Copyright © 1964 by The Reader's Digest Association, Inc. Excerpt from "How to Lick the Hazards of Foul Weather Driving" by Paul W. Kearney. Copyright © 1963 by The National Safety Council.

To *Redbook,* for the excerpt from "Ringo Starr: Domesticated Beatle" by Robert Deardorff.

To Charles Scribner's Sons, for excerpts from the short story "The Killers" in *Men Without Women* by Ernest Hemingway.

To *This Week Magazine,* and the author for "Pitcher Who Paints" by Leslie Lieber. Reprinted from *This Week Magazine.* Copyright © 1965 by the United Newspapers Magazine Corporation.

CONTENTS

actual interview.   Getting the subject to talk freely.
Pitfalls.   Other interviews that relate to the subject
of the article.   Note-taking.   Using a tape recorder.
How to become a good listener.

and expresses his individual approach. Changing
styles with changing times. How awareness of today's world contributes to a writer's use of language.

The literary agent—his role, function, and fees.
His availability to the beginning writer. The query
letter: how to write it; why and when. Examples.
Tips. What to avoid. A writer's working library.
When an editor says "rewrite." The market for new
article writers.

HOW TO WRITE
SUCCESSFUL MAGAZINE ARTICLES

א 1

THE WRITER'S TOOLS

I THINK THE MOST useful advice I have ever given a beginning writer is this: Start immediately to consider yourself a writer. Many young writers are very timid about admitting to themselves and others that they are entering what they feel are the sacred portals of the press.

I was recently discussing with a student an article he had in process concerning some of the dramatic events the moving van people cope with. He had done his library research and had collected a number of case histories. Now he needed to interview the officers of some van lines to check his findings, verify his technical information and collect anecdotes.

"Call the public relations officer of one of the big companies," I advised, "and ask him for an interview."

"But who shall I say I am?"

"Say in a businesslike manner that you are a writer; that you are at work on an article and would like to check with him."

He hesitated, then said, "But how can I say I am a writer if I have never had anything published?"

"You are a writer if you are working seriously and consistently to perfect your craft." (Note: the public relations man did see him and he got his story.)

A way of life

From the moment you say to yourself, "I am a writer," you are opening the doors to a new world for yourself. For writing becomes a way of life, and all you do and see and feel is bent to serve your craft. So acknowledge to yourself, proudly and honestly, that you are a writer, then make your statement come true.

Now, for a few tools of the trade:

1) *Give yourself a time to work.* This may be difficult to arrange if you have a full-time job and are a part-time writer on the side, but it can be done. I know a successful editor who also writes books. He gets up every morning at five o'clock, makes himself a cup of coffee, and goes to his writing until seven, when he dresses for the office and joins his family at breakfast.

I know a mother of young children who gets her brood off to school and keeps the hours from 9:30 to 11:30 in the morning sacred to her writing. I know a public relations man, a bachelor, who is writing a novel. He wakes up every morning at four, wraps himself in a sweater, takes his portable typewriter on his lap, writes until six, then goes back to sleep until eight. And I know others who religiously reserve the time from eight until midnight three nights a week for writing. Jean Kerr says she wrote many of her books while she waited in the car for her children who were at dancing school or Scout meetings. And full-time, professional free-lance writers keep their appointments with the typewriter as religiously as does the engineer with his drawing board, or the lawyer with his clients.

When you have decided on whatever writing time works best with your life, stick to it except in case of a real emergency. Let your friends know that you are not available on the telephone at that time. Once you permit another activity to take over today or something else to nibble at it tomorrow, you are lost.

2) *Give yourself a place to work.* If you have an extra room you can reserve for yourself with a door that closes, you are indeed blessed. But even if you haven't, there are ways to manage.

The actual space can be small. All you need is a table to hold a typewriter, a chair, a shelf for your reference books and some kind of file for your notes. A corrugated box from the grocer's that will hold a collection of file folders upright will do until you want to invest in a cabinet.

One writer I know has made himself such a writing nook by putting up a room divider in his living room with his private corner behind it. Another fenced off space with a large screen. A housewife reserves a corner of her kitchen for writing. Caution: Be sure your writing corner is out of bounds for all the family; you will want to leave your books open and your papers available for your next assault on them.

These seemingly routine matters mark the difference between the amateur and the professional. The amateur works when the mood moves him or in spare time; the professional works in planned time. If you are a housewife, you don't prepare meals only when you are in the mood; you work on a schedule. If you are an engineer, you don't do your calculations in your spare time. So, similarly, if you want to be a writer, you must value your work and assign to it a planned place and time in your day.

3) *Learn to take notes as instinctively as you breathe.* Each year at the first meeting of my class in writing, I say emphatically, "If you are to succeed as a writer, you must keep notebooks." And each time about half the class wearily indicates they've heard that old chestnut before. But, as the months go by, it is invariably the students who have taken up the notebook habit and persevered in it, whose work is finding its way into print.

Two notebooks

I suggest, as a starter, that you have two notebooks: a) an idea notebook, and b) one especially for the article you have in the works at the time. Each writer will find the kind he likes best to use. Some writers like 3 x 5 or 4 x 6 cards. They don't work for me; I lose them and forget to label them. Others like sheets of folded paper they can file later. I have settled for inexpensive 5 x 8 notebooks with spiral bindings and flexible covers from the five-and-ten. This size fits into the usual woman's handbag or a man's pocket. As one is used up, I number it, write the date and subject on the back and file it away.

a) *The idea notebook.* Ideas for articles, colorful bits of conversation, quotations that seem especially pertinent, and even useful facts come to you at odd and unexpected moments. When they do, capture them at once in your idea notebook.

An item in the morning paper suggests a possible article; that reminds you of an observation on a similar subject in your mother-in-law's last letter and both call to mind something that happened to you as a child. At that moment, an article is born, and the whole package is so pat and so vivid you are sure you will never forget it.

You will. A week or a month from now, you may recall the idea but you will have forgotten all the accompanying details that made it come alive. If you have the jotting down in your idea notebook, you have it ready when you want to start your piece. You may even have an opening sentence.

As you pass a school, you hear two little boys having an argument. You are amused by the names they call each other, their turns of expression. Whip out your notebook and get it down. One of these days you may need some "boy talk" and what you invent is likely to sound synthetic; but your notebook will give you rhythm and words.

Perhaps, in the back of your mind, you plan a personal experience piece on your relationship with your child's nursery school teacher. You may find a statistic in a news magazine that would support your own observation. Copy your statistic then and there, putting down the exact words, the author, the date of issue and the page number. If you depend on your memory, you may never find the quote again.

These are only a few examples of the riches your notebook will have stored away. Treat it as if it were a deep freeze with food for dinner tomorrow or next week or next month. Or for next year or even later. You may be of the filing persuasion and want to file your notes in folders, under such headings as ideas, dialogue, etc. Or if you follow my system, you will leave your notes in the numbered or dated books and when you are hungry for ideas, leaf through and find notes you have forgotten that answer your need or start you on a productive train of thought.

A young writer I know came in one late autumn afternoon from a walk over fields covered with a thin sifting of the first tentative snow of the season. He went to his typewriter and spent the next hour capturing the scene—from the sound of the crunch of the freezing stubble under his shoes to the color of the gray early twilight. Finished, it went in his notebook, ready for use when he needed it.

A brilliant example of this sort of note-taking is to be found in the *Notebooks* of the great French writer, Albert Camus (Knopf). They show how this really professional man of letters had trained his eyes to see, his ears to hear and how perceptively he had recorded for future use the sights, sounds and emotions of every day. It might be a description of a North African city, a conversation overheard at a bar, or a conclusion he had reached. These turned up later, in many cases unaltered, in an essay, novel or play. "I don't know of a better book," says *The New York Times* critic, Charles Poore, "to recommend to anyone who is concerned in reading, in writing and in the conjuring wonders that can be performed with the letters of the alphabet."

b) *The notebook for the article you are writing*. When you have decided on a subject for an article, start a new notebook for it. If you are working on two articles at once, have a notebook for each. Use these as your source books. When you find a pertinent fact, a statistic, a quotation or an idea that will advance your story, jot it down immediately. If you telephone someone for information, write down not only what he says, but his telephone number and extension, so that if you need to call him back, you can reach him quickly.

Sometimes when you are writing, you come to a cranky sentence that rolls itself into a knot and refuses to come straight. Finally, you give up on it. Then in the night your subconscious takes over and the words fall into place. With a notebook on your bedside table, you can jot the sentence down and turn over to a peaceful sleep.

If in a book or magazine, you find information you need, note the title, author, date of issue and page number, so that if you need to refer to it again, you can easily locate it. I remember once when I was writing a piece on the pre-Columbian American Indian, I became so absorbed by an account of the centuries-long trek of the Navahos from the Bering Strait to Arizona that I failed to take notes as I went along. When I came to polish my final draft, I was hazy on one fact. It took me two hours to leaf through the book to find the statement. By the time I had located it, I had lost my train of thought and my writing impetus, and half a day was killed before I was back into the swing of my piece.

An equally good reason for keeping complete notes is that after you have submitted your article to an editor, he may want verification. If you can immediately give him the source of your statement, you will have become, in his eyes, an accurate and careful writer. And that is an enviable reputation for any author.

4) *Open your eyes and ears to ideas.* Try the approach of Margaret Cousins, a distinguished and successful writer, now senior editor at Doubleday, formerly managing editor of *Good Housekeeping* and *McCall's.* In an article in *The Writer* (January, 1964) she recalls that when she was a young editor, her chief asked her to submit twenty-five article ideas to him every Monday. "The overwhelming necessity of producing these ideas," she says, "developed in me a habit of awareness, which is now so inculcated that I cannot walk down any street or go anywhere to this day that my mind does not consciously store up impressions, observations, dialogues, attitudes, and a dozen things which could be turned into articles for a magazine."

Twenty-five ideas a week may seem like a formidable number. But let me suggest that you set yourself to finding one article idea a day which you record in your notebook. Some of them will eventually become articles; some will add spice to a piece on another subject; but more important, you will be training your eye and ear. You will be taking part in the life around you and making it your own. You will be giving yourself an exercise in inventiveness, which will make your own living richer and fuller and add the same qualities to your writing.

ℵ 2

READ IT IN THE MAGAZINES

IN THE SUMMER of 1921, a London newsboy sold his papers by calling out, "Caruso's dead. 'e died 'e did. 'ow did 'e die? Read it in the piper, read it in the piper."

He was an astute young merchant. And his pitch might be followed by anyone aspiring to write for today's magazines. In his lead he told just enough to rouse his hearers and to awaken their curiosity; then went right into his text, which, in that case, was the news story in his paper, Caruso's death. He also used rhythmical English and that, too, serves a writer well.

But the reason I cite this little anecdote is that I wish to introduce to you the first step in writing articles for periodicals. That is: find out for yourself what editors —and by the same token, readers—want. How? *Read it in the magazines.*

You would undoubtedly tell me that you do read any number of magazines. But you probably read them in the same fashion that the millions of people for whom the

magazines are edited read them—for interest, for amuse-
ment, for information, for escape. I urge you to read them
as a professional reads them: to discover for yourself what
sorts of subjects are being offered, and to learn how the
skillful writer presents his facts and achieves his effects;
how he communicates his point of view to the reader.

It was my privilege once to have been a member of a
physical exercise class for ladies of odd shapes who were
hoping to achieve more classical figures. It was conducted
by a rangy English woman of force and suasion. "Now
lift your left leg," she would tell her class who were pros-
trate on mats before her. "Next, lower it slowly, thinking
all the while of your abdomen. This exercise is to
strengthen your abdominal muscles, but it will do you
no good unless you think of what you want to accomplish
while you do it."

The same thought may be carried over into our reading
of the current magazines. Just as an exercise student may
thoughtlessly lift and lower her leg and accomplish little
thereby, so you can read half a dozen magazines a day
and give yourself little help with your own writing.

But, beginning now, read for profit. Choose at least one
article a week for study. Select one that you enjoy, about
which you might say, "I wish I had written that." After
you have read it once for pleasure, read it again and then
again and dig out the techniques the author used.

If you have ever watched a painter in an art gallery as
he scans a fellow artist's work, you would see that he
doesn't stop merely at enjoying the picture. He examines
the brush work, he notes the use of light and shadow, the
colors. In his mind, he is holding a brush and following the master's strokes.

As you become a professional writer, you will find yourself doing the same thing as you read. And once you have established the habit of reading and analyzing, you are on the way to establishing your own skills.

As we progress in this book from chapter to chapter, I will suggest writing techniques which you find in the magazines on your own reading tables and which you can adapt to your own use.

Let us begin now by taking a short survey of nine national periodicals. These are leaders and their techniques are largely followed by the hundreds of other journals.

Find in your own collection or in the public library or borrow from friends at least one copy of a recent issue of the following magazines:

McCall's
Ladies' Home Journal
Saturday Evening Post
Look
Redbook
Good Housekeeping
Reader's Digest
A men's magazine, such as *True* or *Argosy*
A pace-setter such as *Harper's* or *The Atlantic*

Begin by counting the kinds of articles in each magazine. Take a sheet of ruled paper for each publication—I use a long, ruled yellow pad and list each article in the issue. Pass up the fiction for the moment and also, in the women's magazines, disregard what are known as "service" articles: those devoted to food, home building and decoration, housekeeping, fashion and beauty. These service articles are almost always prepared by staff editors and are rarely bought from free-lance writers.

For our purpose we will classify the remaining articles in each magazine in three categories:

1. About people: the personal experience and human interest pieces, interviews, profiles, etc., also those in which people are used as examples.

2. About things: these may cover anything from traffic on the highways to the atom bomb.

3. About ideas or opinions: these range from marriage and divorce to public affairs.

So at the top of your sheet of paper, put three headings: *people, things, ideas and opinions* (this last as one column). As you read each article, put in the appropriate column a number—1, 2, or 3—the classification into which the article falls.

You will find that many articles come under all three headings: for instance, an article on traffic in New York might include an interview with the traffic commissioner or bystanders or taxi drivers, in other words, *people.* It is about a *thing,* traffic. And it will probably offer a solution, the author's or an authority's, which would be an *idea* or an *opinion.*

Human interest

As you make such a detailed analysis, you may find yourself in for some surprises. You will probably find more articles on public affairs than you had imagined and more thoughtful consideration given to today's human and civic and governmental problems. But you will also discover that you have more numbers 1, 2, or 3 in your column on people than in either of the other two, and sometimes more than the other two combined.

In other words, today's magazines are largely about people; and events and things are presented in terms of people. A recent issue of *Look* had only articles about people. One issue of *The Saturday Evening Post* was about equally divided between people on the one hand and ideas and things on the other. *Redbook* and *Good Housekeeping* have monthly articles on personal experiences. Out of forty articles in one issue of *Reader's Digest,* twenty-two were either personal experience or human interest. A quick rundown of titles will show that at once. Here are a few:

Lightning Strikes Bugaboo Spire (a story of mountain climbers)
What Women Can Do for Peace
A Second Chance for George (on retraining for jobs, with special reference to one man)
I Enjoy Myself Most When I'm Scared
They Discover America
I Remember Hyde Park
My Most Unforgettable Character
Around the World with Bob Hope
How to Handle a Hot Potato (personal experience)
My Night as a Police Officer
When the World Is Too Much with You
Ask Henry (the story of a boy columnist)
Something Special in Vacations
Don Eugenio Shows the Way (a Brazilian businessman's story)
The Greatest African Explorer (Stanley)

In *McCall's* and the *Ladies' Home Journal,* almost every article, including the service pieces, is either "I" or "you" or "she."

Why should a writer accept the verdict of the large circulation magazines as a gauge of what readers want?

Because the large circulation magazines are very sensitive to the desires—and as time goes on, the changing desires—of their readers. The publishers are well-financed and can afford to keep research staffs to make surveys to discover what readers like in each issue. These surveys are often arranged by age, education, or income groupings of readers. (Does the twenty-to-thirty group have different interests from those of older people?)

The editors are looking for new ideas, and since they publish a variety of articles, they can do a certain amount of experimenting. Also, they have correspondents and writers throughout the country reporting on developments that would be of interest. These are publications you will eventually want to write for, and you have a personal interest in seeing what they are publishing.

Why should a writer study the styles and techniques of contributors to the large circulation magazines? Aren't there better patterns for style and techniques?

In the first place, the large circulation magazines can afford to pay a writer well for his work. Therefore, the editors can seek out able craftsmen, good reporters, writers who are full of ideas and skillful in presenting people and things and opinions through words. The writers for these journals have completed their apprenticeship and have learned how to present their subjects with clarity and how to attract and hold the attention of the reader.

This is not to say that the new writer should devote himself solely to the large circulation periodicals. He will also want to round out his reading through books and other magazines.

ℵ 3

EDITORS LIKE PEOPLE

IF YOU ARE A doubting Thomas who can't trust the evidence of your own Gallup poll which indicates that today's editors like to populate their articles with real people, do take a look at the market lists. These are published in magazines for writers and in books such as *The Writer's Handbook*. They list the current magazines, and under each listing the editor tells what he is looking for from writers.

McCall's asks for "articles that reach a surprising or dramatic conclusion, personality pieces about special people, unusual or first-person narratives."

Argosy: "Profiles of unusual male personalities."

Good Housekeeping: "Especially interested in first-person experiences in the fields of human relations, individual achievement, practical living, romance and social techniques."

Look: "Articles on people who mean something to other

18

people. Warmth, understanding and information. Prefer them focused on people rather than things."

Family Circle: "Inspirational articles about people with a sound and satisfying philosophy of family living; factual stories that partake of the excitement, humor and emotion of a good fiction piece."

Family Weekly: "Emphasis upon individuals, famous or in the news, adding depth or unknown facts with anecdotal or personal experience approach."

The religious publications are also hospitable to personality pieces. *The Christian Herald* likes "human interest articles with religious, educational or social implications," and *The Catholic Digest* asks for "articles on leading Catholic personalities."

Even business and trade journals take pleasure in printing success stories of business people who have shown ingenuity or diligence or inventiveness, whether it is in selling shoes or setting up computers.

As a result, in the last fifteen years, we have seen an increase in profiles, human interest and personal experience articles; even purely factual articles are often told through an interview with some authority or illustrated with anecdote and dialogue.

This has meant that much non-fiction writing has become narrative writing, important for the writer in that it calls for two kinds of skills: the successful writer must still be a good reporter—he must have his facts, all his facts—more facts than he will use. He must know where to go for these facts and how to use them. But he will also need a number of skills that have heretofore been the province of the writer of fiction: how to present a character, how to tell a story and how to handle dialogue.

The result is that today's article writer has a more en-
joyable role than ever before. He has the satisfaction
that comes from passing on information, plus the creative
pleasure of writing about people.

This change in the character of non-fiction has been accompanied by a new line-up on the contents pages of
our popular magazines. *McCall's Magazine* for April, 1946,
to cite one instance, listed six short stories and one novel,
very few general articles. Fiction accounted for the greater
number of pages in the issue. Five years later, there were
four short stories and one serial. The June, 1966, issue
listed three stories—and eighteen non-fiction features, plus
fourteen service articles on food, fashion, home decoration,
etc. Other popular magazines have followed the same pattern.

The *Ladies' Home Journal* for January, 1946, published
five short stories and one novel; its June, 1966, issue had
only two stories. The *Saturday Evening Post* for April 6,
1946, had four short stories, one novelette and two serials;
for June 18, 1966, it listed one short story and part one of
a two-part serial. During the same twenty-year period, the
number of national magazines carrying fiction has de-
creased.

What we have witnessed is a decline in magazine fiction,
and as fiction has declined, the human interest article
has rushed in to fill the space. The thoughtful writer will
want to know why.

One reason may be the type of fiction that used to be
offered, much of it stereotyped, known in magazine circles as "the formula story": a) boy meets girl, boy
loses girl, boy gets girl; b) the mother-in-law story; c) the
pathetic character; d) the sweet little homebody wife who

always managed to keep her husband when the siren from the city appeared. The ending was usually happy and the solution pat. Many readers may have felt it was too pat. Then, too, radio and later television brought soap operas, western stories and movies into the home, which may have satisfied those who once read merely for escape.

Life was increasingly full of problems. Since World War II, we have lived in the shadow of the atom bomb; war seems always at our doorstep. In our own country, we have become involved in racial tensions. Even in our private lives, many of our long-held beliefs have faltered; juvenile delinquency has appeared in our own homes and those of our neighbors. We have been shocked to discover that our beautiful, well-nourished children are not as physically fit as other children in the Western world. Sexual standards have changed.

As a result, "happy" formula fiction was no longer as satisfying as it had been. Nor did the average reader find much more satisfaction in the intellectual fiction which began to appear, written by the angry young men and the equally angry young women who could find nothing good in the world.

Human interest articles

The great reading public wanted more realism than popular fiction had given them, less misery than the intellectual writers handed out. They also wanted heroes and heroines. They wanted to feel that real people had met the problems they were facing and had found some sort of solution. So the fact story, that is, the story of real people, moved in to answer the need.

I doubt that many editors analyzed this change in fashion

at the time. Through their reader research they discovered that fiction wasn't as popular as it had been. The few human interest articles they published were widely read.

The Reader's Digest, which over in its corner was growing like corn in Kansas, was printing articles about real people. Its series, *My Most Unforgettable Character,* was one of its most popular features. Marc A. Rose, then senior editor, had this to say in *The Writer's Handbook* on what the *Digest* was looking for:

> The most popular, hence the most salable and highest-priced article known to us, is the kind variously called "the art of living essay," the "self-help" piece, the "uplift piece" . . .
>
> "How to Be Happy Though Married."
>
> "How to Conquer Fear"—or bashfulness, or self-consciousness or what have you.
>
> The bulk of such articles are bilge . . . but the best . . . are superb and beyond price. . . .
>
> Personality articles rank high. Again their value is measured by applicability. How did this man succeed? Are there hints for me in his career? . . . Everyone wants to know how to be loved, how to win money or fame or power, how to stay healthy. . . .
>
> Social progress articles—the community that solved a race problem; the farmers who licked the boll weevil; the cop who abolished juvenile delinquency on his beat—these are always marketable. Again, it must be not a narrow, local situation, but one of wide interest.
>
> Aim at the broadest human appeal, which means getting as close as you can to the reader's self-interest. . . .
>
> Here, just for fun, I have drawn up titles for six possible treatments of the same general set of facts:

1. The Economics of the Automobile Industry
2. Great Fortunes in America, a Study
3. American Millionaires
4. How Henry Ford Got Rich
5. How I Got Rich, by Henry Ford
6. How You Can Get Rich

Do I have to point out the scale of ascending appeal?

The *Ladies' Home Journal*, beginning as early as 1940, had run into a gold mine with its "How America Lives" —stories of real families. *McCall's*, after the war, published "A *McCall's* Personal Story" and "This Is How I Keep House," also accounts of the experiences of actual persons. The first articles on preserving a marriage were appearing. Even magazines addressed to men were presenting on their sports pages stories of real athletes. And as editors discovered that these human interest pieces were popular, they published more of them and less fiction. It was as simple as that.

More often than not, these articles concern personalities one would not call glamorous. This is not to say that the love affair of a princess or of a television or Hollywood personality doesn't have great drawing power; it does. But stories of just people—small businessmen, women who live in split-level houses, school teachers, bus conductors—can also attract and satisfy the reader. These are people with whom we can identify, men and women whose problems are our problems.

Although there is often an inspirational note, and courage and perseverance are usually ingredients, these stories do not always have a conventionally happy ending.

The subject may still be living with his or her disability or shyness; the boy who didn't get to college may not have become the president of the company. The woman who was losing her husband to the siren or his secretary may have been able to win him back, but the patches on the marriage still show; or she may have lost him and is facing life alone with her children. But our hero (or heroine) has learned to live with the problem. In some way he has come through. And his story leaves the reader with the hope that what he has done I, too, can do. Life is worth living and there are compensations.

One more example: a poll of readers of a recent issue of a popular women's magazine showed that twice as many people read a personal experience article as read a novel by a best-selling author. I don't think this means that fiction is about to disappear. It does mean that the emphasis today is on non-fiction, and the statistics show which way the wind is blowing.

Nor does what I have said indicate that only human interest pieces are being published today. The news magazines and journals of opinion are still attracting readers. Even popular magazines devote space to purely factual articles that do not focus on personalities, although such articles are usually newsworthy and on subjects of high interest to the reader. The think piece and the essay still have their place.

Non-fiction narrative

A corollary to the trend in magazine articles is found in the book field, where the non-fiction narrative style long ago made its way into history and biography.

We might cite Homer as the originator of narrative history—he was read as fiction for centuries until the dis-covery of the ruins of Troy and of Agamemnon's palace showed that his narrative, embroidered as it was over the ages, was based solidly on fact. And there was that gad-about historian, Herodotus. In our own time, Cleveland Amory, reviewing Barbara Tuchman's *The Proud Tower* (*Cosmopolitan,* February, 1966), speaks of her "history-telling talents." And we have Cornelius Ryan's *The Last Battle.*

Many biographies based on fact have been written with a storyteller's skill. Plutarch comes to mind, and centuries later Lytton Strachey's *Eminent Victorians.* Lillian Ross combined excellent reportage with fictional skills in *Portrait of Hemingway.*

The non-fiction narrative book reached another turning point when fiction writer Truman Capote, after five years of factual research, brought out *In Cold Blood,* which he called a "new literary form: the non-fiction novel." What-ever doubts we may have as to its "newness," it is a brilliant example of what can be accomplished in readability by the combination of a skillful fiction technique with the careful and copious research of a good reporter.

What this adds up to for today's non-fiction writer is very simple. He needs two kinds of skill: that of the re-porter to dig out facts, and that of the fiction writer to make his piece interesting. Neither is difficult to acquire. And there is the added incentive of an expanding market for non-fiction, with more than a thousand publications in the United States buying articles, and six articles appear-ing in print for every one piece of fiction.

❧ 4

RESEARCH—DIGGING OUT THE FACTS

EDITORS' OUTGOING MAIL BASKETS are filled with manuscripts going back to authors who have not done a thorough enough job of digging for facts. One of my less than happy experiences as an editor concerned an article manuscript which on first reading seemed a natural. The theme of the piece was that a product in common household use had dangerous side effects. The authority cited by the author was reputable, the information promised to be of value to our readers, and the manuscript was interesting and well written. Since the writer was not one of our regulars, I turned the manuscript over to our staff for checking.

My mood was that of a smug and self-satisfied editor who had discovered a new writer. But the mood did not last. Our research department found that the manufacturer of the product had already corrected most of the defects, that there were other aspects of its use which the author of the article had not troubled to investigate. Once we learned this, every statement in the article had to be so qualified that there was no point in publishing it, and we dropped it. We also dropped the writer. The information our staff turned up was readily available to the author if he had taken the trouble to look for it. His research was sloppy.

This is not an unusual case—and all the while the magazines are scanning the horizon for new writers who are dependable. The key word here is *dependable*. The professional writers whose names you see over and over in one publication after another have earned a reputation for being thorough and accurate. Not all magazines have research departments. Those that do not, must depend on the writer, and it is to the credit of careful research by writers that so few errors of fact find their way into print.

I should like to see posted over the typewriter of every aspiring writer the statement that research is the first essential; facts are the foundation on which any article is built. This is just as true of today's narrative non-fiction as it was and is of the purely factual article.

"The difference between a $75 article and a $750 article," says Nannine Joseph, literary agent, "is exactly how much research has been done and how much the author really knows about the subject and how much authority shows through." Marc Rose, late senior editor of *The Reader's Digest,* advised writers to gather twice as much material as they will use, "so that a selection can be made from a wealth of material." He held that if your facts are scanty your article will be thin.

Setting yourself up as a fact-finding private eye is not as difficult as it may seem. Once you start looking into your subject, you find your curiosity aroused; you are an explorer in new territory, and sometimes it is hard to stop researching and start writing.

You get your facts from print and from people. You use both.

Libraries

The first step in gleaning facts from print is to take your public library into partnership. Unless you already know your nearest library as well as your own living room, make a special get-acquainted tour and ask the librarian to help you locate the following for future use:

The Readers' Guide to Periodical Literature. This is published monthly and bound yearly. It lists the subjects covered in more than a hundred selected periodicals and is indexed by title, subject, and author's name. It also includes the names and dates of the magazines in which the articles have appeared. Therefore, you can easily consult particular issues to see how a subject has been treated— the tone, approach, emphasis—and you can then decide whether the idea you have in mind is original enough to justify another article.

The Cumulative Book Index does for books what the *Readers' Guide* does for periodicals.

The New York Times Index will tell you whether a subject was covered in *The Times* and will give the date the item appeared there and the page number. If your library does not have a file of *The Times* (bound or on microfilm), the date in the *Index* will give you a clue that may help you find out whether your local papers carried the news story.

Then locate *Who's Who in America* for short biographical sketches of prominent living people; *Current Biogra-*

phy for longer accounts; and the *Dictionary of American Biography* for information on Americans who are no longer living. The British *Who's Who* lists British and internationally famous people. Know where to find the *World Almanac* or the *Information Please Almanac* for statistics and offbeat facts, and the encyclopedias and reference books. Many libraries have what is called a vertical file for pamphlets, clippings, etc. Ask the librarian for the folder on the subject you are interested in.

If your local library does not have the reference books you need, there may be a college library nearby that you can use. Your local library can usually get books and bound volumes of magazines from other libraries on an exchange basis, or it may be able to get photostats of material that is too valuable to lend.

Whenever you are stuck, ask your librarian for help. I have worked with librarians in cities, villages and universities, and I have never found one who did not have a rich fund of information which he was eager to share. Librarians love their books, they love research, know sources of information and will take a personal interest in your project.

I remember, especially, a young man in the music room of the New York Public Library to whom I appealed for help on a piece I was assigned to write on a violinist, well-known in Europe, who had recently come to New York. The librarian knew the musician's work through recordings and supplied me with clippings of reviews of his European concerts. He gave me a little history of the man's professional life and his style of playing. When I went for my interview with the great man, I had been so well briefed that I was able to begin our talk on a friendly

basis, to ask intelligent questions and to lead him into anecdotes that made all the difference between a dull piece and
a lively one.

The Government Printing Office

Another excellent source of information is the Government Printing Office in Washington, D.C., which can supply free or inexpensive source books and pamphlets on
practically every subject under the sun. Other sources include business and industrial firms, professional societies,
Congressmen, museums and trade magazines. Politicians
and other celebrities often have press agents who are only
too glad to supply information on their clients.

Let's follow the sort of research from printed material
you would do on a hypothetical article. Suppose an important citizen of your state has become prominent in politics and is about to run for Congress. He is a self-made
man and, while the papers have been full of news about
him, you have seen little about his years at State University. Perhaps there is an article there and you would
like to write it.

All the reading you do for research purposes should be
done swiftly and selectively. Go through the printed material quickly, making notes of what you may find useful and
discarding other items. But do get down your dates and
the book and page numbers of anything you may want to
refer to again.

Your first port of call would probably be the library,
where you would consult *Who's Who in America* and *Current Biography* to give you dates and a quick look at his
life. Next, the *Readers' Guide to Periodical Literature* and
the *Cumulative Book Index*. As you scan the magazines

and any books listed on your hero, you will learn whether his activities while he was in college have been well or recently covered. If so, you will probably decide that you should get a new focus for your article—or drop it. If you still feel that you have an article, you read on to inform yourself fully about his life and background.

Then concentrate on the years when he was in college. Your reading has given you the dates. As you take a quick run through the papers for those years, you learn what was going on in the world then that might have influenced the young man; also whether his college was in the news. And you look over back files of your local papers for the same purpose.

Look up copies of his high school and college yearbooks to see their comments on him. Did he show any particular talents? Was he active in sports or any other campus activity? If he is now a member of a business firm, they may have releases on him, his promotions and rise in the company; his political party will undoubtedly have a sheaf of material on him. In the meantime, you are scanning the newspapers and magazines to keep an eye on what he is up to now.

By this time you feel that you know him well. You also know the gaps in your information. You are ready to interview him, his associates, teachers or classmates. You have enough clues to be ready with questions.

Specialized research techniques

The amount of research necessary for an informative article usually comes as a shock to beginning writers. Advertising writers and newspaper reporters, who think it would be nice to take a flyer into the greener fields of the magazines, are not only shocked but incredulous. Often they have succeeded in their own fields and think it should be a snap to turn out an article.

The ad writer knows how to say much in a few colorful, telling phrases. He takes information about a product from the manufacturer without question, plays with words and ideas and slogans and comes up with short, effective selling copy. When he tackles an article, he brings to it the same naive belief in a product's good qualities. All you have to do, he thinks, is tell the reader how good it tastes, how easy it is to use, how beautiful, attractive and magnetic it will make her or him. Instead of a hundred-word ad, he writes a two-thousand-word ad. It isn't an article.

The newspaper reporter has leads to innumerable stories. He often writes direct, clear-headed, straight-thinking and hard-hitting prose. But when he goes out to cover a fire or a political speech, an accident or a police court, he writes what he sees and makes the next edition. For a Sunday paper he may take a little time to acquaint himself with the background of the subject. He makes no attempt to cover it in depth. When he comes to write for a magazine, he does the same superficial work. And he wonders why his pieces are returned.

Both the ad writer and the reporter took plenty of time to learn the techniques of the kinds of writing they have succeeded in. They should also take time to study the wholly different techniques they need to turn out articles. But these gifted people who do take time to master magazine techniques—the research, the writing and rewriting and revising and polishing—come to the top of the heap. Think of onetime ad-man Gerald Carson, ex-reporters

Paul Gallico, John Gunther, Quentin Reynolds, Marguerite Higgins.

To give you a picture of how a professional free-lance writer gathers facts, I am reprinting an article by John Kord Lagemann, whose articles appear regularly in leading national magazines. Following the article, Mr. Lagemann tells how he wrote it and lists the different kinds of research that went into this one short piece. (The article originally appeared in *The Reader's Digest* of March, 1953 and was reprinted with his notes by the Society of Magazine Writers in *A Guide to Successful Magazine Writing*.)

YOU'RE SMARTER THAN YOU THINK

by John Kord Lagemann

"Women know everything," my grandfather once told me, "and Heaven help us if they ever find it out."

He was referring, of course, to feminine intuition—that mysterious faculty which enables women to answer questions before they're asked; predict the arrival of unexpected guests; identify social climbers, alcoholics and rivals as if they were plainly labeled; know without being told when their husbands have quarreled with the boss or daydreamed—just daydreamed, mind you—about another woman.

Ever since Eve took the first bite out of the apple, man has been asking woman how she knows all these things without any apparent reason for knowing. Nothing infuriates him more than to be told: "I just know, that's all."

Does intuition really exist? And if so, is it feminine? I decided to put the question to science.

Intuition, I learned, is a normal and highly useful function of human intelligence. This fact has been confirmed by each of the half dozen authorities I consulted. Though associated with high IQs in both sexes, it is more characteristic of women than of men.

Why? As Dr. Helene Deutsch, author of *The Psychology of Women,* points out, in adolescence a boy is interested primarily in asserting himself in action, while a girl's interests center around feelings, her own and others. Dr. Deutsch compares the adolescent girl to "someone listening in the dark and perceiving every noise with special acuteness." From the understanding she gains of her own emotions she is able by analogy to relive the emotions of others.

Women don't pay nearly as much attention as men to what people say, but they are apt to know a great deal more about the way people feel. One winter when I was living in New Hampshire my friend Mr. White coveted a corner pasture which his neighbor Mr. Perry stubbornly refused to sell. The men were no longer on speaking terms, but their wives went right on visiting over the phone. One night after a long and rambling party-line visit—in which the land issue was never mentioned—Mrs. White said to her husband, "I think Mr. Perry will sell that corner lot if you still want it." When I saw the Whites a few months later the deal had been completed.

Reduced to simplest terms intuition is a way of thinking without words—a short cut to the truth, and in matters of emotion, the only way of getting there at all. Dr. Carl Jung defines it as "a basic psychological function which transmits perceptions in an unconscious way." This perception is based on the evidence of our physical senses. But because it taps knowledge and experience of which we aren't aware it is often confused with telepathy, clairvoyance or extrasensory perception. We all know the "psychic" card player who seems to read another's hand; actually he notes a telltale flutter of your eyelid or lip, a hesitation in speech, the tightening of a wrist muscle when your hand touches a card. He may not be aware himself of the clues he follows.

Civilization has substituted words and various other abstractions for the direct experience of seeing, hearing, smelling, tasting, touching and feeling. But our neglected senses still go right on operating, far better than we realize. Take the sense of smell, perhaps the least developed of the senses. We used to laugh at backwoods doctors who diagnosed certain diseases by sniffing the air near the patient. Then we discovered that these diseases really did produce chemical changes resulting in characteristic odors. Experiments have shown that the odor of a person's breath actually varies with changes in his emotional attitude. The distance over which we can unconsciously pick up the scent of another human being is unknown, but it is almost certainly greater than the length of a room. How can an odor of which you are not even aware mean anything to you? If you've ever been awakened slowly and deliciously by the aroma of coffee and bacon, you know the answer.

Last summer I saw an example of how the senses coöperate to produce intuition. On the boat from Woods Hole to Martha's Vineyard my wife nodded toward a young woman sitting near-by and remarked, "I'm sure I know her. Yet I can't remember having seen her before."

Impulsively we introduced ourselves and mentioned my wife's feeling. After the young woman had spoken, my wife said, "Now I know. You take phone calls for Dr. Miller."

"Why, yes, I do," the girl answered.

Why did my wife feel there was something familiar about the girl? "But don't you see?" she explained to me later. "She *looked* just the way she sounded over the phone." Simple as that. Come to think of it, though, can't almost any teen-ager spot a blind date from the way he or she sounded on the phone?

Most women are quite good at guessing age, particularly if the subject is another woman. If you don't believe it, try it sometime at a party. The difference between a girl of 23 and a girl of 25 is far too subtle to put into words. Men try to reason it out and usually their guesses are not better than chance or gallantry will allow. Yet with the aid of almost imperceptible clues women can often spot the difference.

One of the few attempts to observe intuition systematically was made by Dr. Eric Berne, a former staff psychiatrist with the Army Medical Corps, now a practicing psychoanalyst at Carmel, Calif. While interviewing men at an Army Separation Center, Dr. Berne and his colleagues tried to guess, before the patient had spoken, what his occupation had been in civilian life. All the patients were dressed in standard maroon bathrobes and cloth slippers. The doctors' guesses averaged well above chance. "On one occasion," Dr. Berne reports, "the occupations of 26 successive men were guessed correctly." Clues unconsciously detected in the men's eyes, gestures, facial expressions, speech, hands, and so on, probably explain this success.

As psychiatry and common sense have actually proved, you know a lot more than you are aware that you know. The mind tunes into consciousness only a few of the impressions which flow in from your sense organs. But your brain does not waste these impulses. It stores them up in your unconscious mind where they are ready to be used. Some physicians, for instance, have only to glance at a patient to diagnose correctly a disease which others cannot identify without painstaking examination. These intuitive doctors note many faint clues and match them with relevant information accumulated over a lifetime of experience.

Likewise, every intuitive person knows how to drag on his reserve of unconscious knowledge and experience in coping with the problems of everyday life. The American Chemical Society questioned 232 leading U. S. scientists, found that 83 per cent of them depended on intuition in their research after intense conscious effort had failed to produce results. A similar study by Dr. Eliot Dole Hutchinson revealed that intuition played an important part in the creative work of 80 per cent of a sample of 253 artists, musicians and writers.

The unconscious part of your brain never stops working. So when you're faced with a perplexing job, work on it as hard as you can. Then if you can't lick it, try sleeping on it or taking a walk or relaxing with friends. If you have primed yourself with all available facts, the answer is likely to "dawn" on you while your mind is seemingly at rest.

In the case of a purely personal decision, the important facts are your own deep feelings, and in this case you know intuitively what to do without the need for long preliminary deliberation. Dr. Sigmund Freud once told a friend, "When making a decision of minor importance I have always found it advantageous to consider all the pros and cons. In vital matters, however, such as the choice of a mate or a profession, the decision should come from the unconscious, from somewhere within ourselves. In the important decisions of our personal lives we should be governed, I think, by the deep inner needs of our nature."

Life is much more interesting for the intuitive person than for the nonintuitive. People mean more when you understand them from the inside out—and because of this, you mean more to them. That is what intuition is, really—finding new and deeper meanings in people and events, making more sense out of life. How can you develop your intuitive powers? Like any other form of thinking, intuition requires an alertness, sensitivity and discipline of mind which have to be cultivated.

Take off the blinders of habit and open your mind to what's going on around you. See people as they really are, not as you think they ought to be. Don't let prejudices distort your vision. Half the trick is to let people tell you about themselves unconsciously. The way a person stands, sits, shakes hands, smokes or sips a drink will be, to the intuitive man or woman, important clues in sizing up character.

Intuition isn't the enemy, but the ally of reason. Effective realistic thinking requires a combination of both.

HOW I WROTE IT

by John Kord Lagemann

The idea for this article actually came from my wife—or rather from my curiosity to find out how she usually happens to know things which I have to spend a long while figuring out—if I ever do.

The notion of writing it came to me two summers ago when I made a flying trip to Europe on very short notice. Betzy's never been to Europe but again and again in her letters she wrote as if she had actually shared in many of my experiences. When I asked her later how she knew what I'd done or felt in such and such a place she said: "It isn't that I knew you did—but that I knew you would."

In our family we have a name for Betzy's intuitive flashes—we call them "Tuthill-isms" after her maiden name. When she gets "that feeling" about a person or situation I still argue with her but I find myself acting on her hunch, even while I'm putting up a show of opposition. I'm sure other husbands have had the same experience.

My first idea was to write a story that would make an appeal for greater acknowledgment of personal feelings in our dealings with one another—not only in domestic life but among our friends and even among business and professional acquaintances. I was going to call it "Let's Get Personal" and show among other things how being personal in this sense helps a physician heal his patient and a good boss get the best out of his staff. It's a piece I still hope to write when I get around to the bulging folder of research stuff that's accumulated on it.

There is nothing original about the idea of writing an article on intuition. I knew, of course, that no magazine editor could buy my intention of writing such a piece or express any definite interest without seeing at least a rough first draft. Intuition is one of a very large category of "essay" subjects which are necessarily almost purely speculative and can only be undertaken under the impetus of personal curiosity.

The research on this one took a lot longer than I had guessed it would. Naturally I was busy on other assignments during the weeks and months I spent on it. The first step was to read everything I could find on the subject at the N. Y. Public Library, the N. Y. Academy of Medicine and the library of the N. Y. State Psychiatric Institute. Altogether I must have looked through about 40 books on psychology, psychiatry, psychoanalysis, personal memoirs and biographies. In addition to the books I looked up scores of references in medical and psychiatric journals. It's surprising how little has been written specifically on intuition as a human phenomenon, probably because it's impossible to deal with it in exact, scientific terms.

While I was still ransacking the libraries I began calling live authorities—teachers and doctors at universities, hospitals and private offices. All told I had about a dozen interviews, about half at informal social gatherings and the rest in offices or laboratories or clinics. It is one of the occupational hazards of the medical and teaching professions to be extremely useful to free-lance writers and most teachers and doctors are extremely generous in giving their time—if they feel that their help will actually count in enlightening not only the writer but his readers as well.

For months I introduced the subject of intuition into conversations with friends or even with people I met for the first time at social gatherings. I discovered that on intuition, as on sex, everybody is an authority. I met hardly anyone who didn't believe in his intuitive powers or have an anecdote or two or three about his experiences along this line.

While I was still researching, interviewing or just talking with people, I was also pounding out notes on the typewriter, fitting them into subdivisions and making stabs now and then at a lead which would establish the printed tone of voice of the final piece. Some sounded pompous (even though I didn't feel that way), others were objectionably argumentative, cute, confidential or what-not. Finally one night after getting home late from a double-feature I wandered to the typewriter and without any intention of working, sat down and wrote down something I remembered hearing my grandfather say when I was a child. When this first paragraph was down I knew I had a lead and next day I was well into the writing.

Up till now I didn't have any definite magazine in mind. The following week I discussed the piece with the editor of a women's magazine, and sent him the first draft. A couple of weeks later he wrote that he was interested in the piece but that it would need to be re-angled for a specific category of woman reader. I fooled around with the piece for another couple of weeks, tightening, fitting in more illustrative anecdotes and trying to get more warmth into it. But this didn't seem to narrow it down any more specifically to a particular sex or category of reader. I called the editor and told him I'd like to try the *Digest*—which I did with his best wishes. Three days later senior editor Charles W. Ferguson called to tell me he liked the piece very much and that he might have more news on it soon. A week later he called again to tell me the *Digest* was buying it for the March issue.

ℵ 5

THE INTERVIEW

ONE OF THE MOST persuasive interviewers I have known is John Kord Lagemann whose article we reprinted in the last chapter. I met him first in Philadelphia where we were both looking over an urban renewal project he was to cover for *McCall's*. As the director of the project took me from house to house on my own exploratory tour, I would find Mr. Lagemann deep in conversation with one or another of the people who lived there. In one house he was sharing a cup of coffee at the kitchen table of one of the ladies.

She was telling him not only what she liked and didn't like about the remodeling but what her husband thought and what it meant to her children. Both were enjoying their chat, and the article he wrote captured the spirit of the people and was made lively with anecdotes and quotes. The reader came to share the pleasure of the people in their remodeled homes.

Mr. Lagemann and I returned to New York and had

dinner on the train. It was only after I had reached home that I realized that during those two hours on the train I had done most of the talking. He had led me on so sympathetically that I had told him my opinions not only on city planning, but on many other things as well.

His skill as an interviewer came from good manners and good humor, a lively curiosity and a very real interest in people and ideas. These are four qualities that will stand any interviewer in good stead.

You will probably interview someone on practically every piece you write. The only exception might be a personal experience of your own; even then you may want to check your memory with someone who has shared the experience.

But aside from the "it happened to me" piece, your interviews fall into two classes: 1) the interview you do for the factual article, and 2) the interview for the profile or human interest piece. Often the two overlap, so keep in mind the purpose of your article.

What to look for

For the factual article, your aim is to obtain information from someone who is an authority. If, for instance, you are writing on the influence of cholesterol on heart disease and your interviewee is a medical man, your aim is to get from him the facts as he has discovered them. Or, you may have gathered information from your reading or some other sources and want to check with him for accuracy. Since you will want to inform your reader—and the editor—that your man is an authority on his subject, you will devote a sentence or so to telling of his professional standing; but his quirks of personality are not important.

If, however, he has reached his conclusions in some unusual manner, you may want to tell the reader what led him to devote himself to that research; then his personality traits may be relevant.

But, by and large, in interviewing just for facts, you don't care whether he is shy or aggressive.

On the other hand when you are interviewing for a profile, then the person interviewed becomes an end in himself, and those traits of his personality which led him to his present state are important.

As an example, we may take the hypothetical case of the distinguished citizen (introduced in the last chapter) who is aspiring to national office and your proposed piece on his college years. You have done all your research from printed materials and are ready to meet him face to face to form your own opinion of him and to get to know him as a human being. Your next step is to ask for an appointment. You may do this either by telephone or by letter.

If your man is someone in your town whom you know even slightly and who knows you, a telephone call may be sufficient. You will identify yourself, say that you are a free-lance writer, tell him something about your proposed article and ask if you may come to see him at his convenience. If you don't know him, write a letter. An experienced writer often feels that it is only good manners to write and so give his subject time to think the matter over and suit his convenience about the time of an appointment.

In your letter, tell him who you are and mention any previous writing experience you may have had. If you have an assignment, tell him where the article will be published. If you are a beginning writer with no published work, say, "I am a free-lance writer" and go on to tell him what your article is about and what information you want from him. Finally, ask him where he'd prefer to meet with you and what time would be most convenient for him. Enclose a stamped, addressed envelope for a reply or say that you will telephone him in a couple of days to set up the appointment.

Keep your letter friendly and businesslike so he will feel he will not be wasting his time. Include a sentence that would give him the feeling that what he says is important. Here is the sort of letter you might write to your aspiring Senator:

Dear Mr. Blank,

I have been following your campaign to represent our state in Congress and was especially interested in your speech on education, in Fayettesville last week and your feeling that college should be brought within reach of all.

I am a free-lance writer and have been contributing regularly to the Sunday magazine of the Whattown *Herald.* I should like to write an article on your own college days at State University, showing how your own schooling may have influenced your present opinions. The —— *Magazine* has expressed an interest in the article.

In these days when entrance into college is difficult, when there are so many college and high school dropouts, I feel that your experience would be helpful and encouraging to high school and college students and to their parents.

May I come to see you at your convenience? I will call your office on Wednesday to ask for an appointment.

Sincerely,

A letter written by one of my students asking for an appointment with a psychiatrist went like this:

Dear Dr. Blank,

My personal physician, Dr. James Brown, has recommended you as "the soundest psychiatrist in New York" and especially knowledgeable on the problems of young people.

I am a free-lance writer and am working on an article on teen-age marriages and their chances of success. I am also a high school teacher and have followed some of these early marriages at first hand, and have talked with young couples, their parents, ministers and social workers.

I should like to interview you at your convenience on the psychiatrist's point of view. I plan to take not more than thirty minutes of your time to ask you some questions on which I would quote you. You may, of course, check your quotes for accuracy, once the article is written.

In a few days, etc., etc.

If you are interviewing someone who has been through a tragic or harrowing experience, express your sympathy. One writer who was asking for an interview from a woman whose son had been killed in a Southern race tragedy, included the following in her letter:

I have followed closely the newspaper accounts of your son's death and have admired your strength and courage throughout. I believe you feel that your son's death was not in vain, and I understand this is a sad period for you. But I feel that your words can give strength to others and to the nation.

In any case, don't let your letter be apologetic. Even an inexperienced writer can often get an interview with very important people.

Do's and don'ts

Now for the interview. Before you go, review the notes you have taken in your research from print. The more you know about your subject to begin with the better your interview is likely to be. Jot down three or four questions you will want to ask him—more if you like.

Be on time and keep the conversation as relaxed as possible. If you are interviewing a busy authority from whom you wish facts and opinions, you can usually start right in with your questions. When you interview the subject of a profile, your first purpose is to establish rapport with him, and you might open the conversation with a question on some subject you know he is interested in. If he's a great fisherman, what luck has he had recently? If you have read something he has written or heard a speech he has made, say you were especially interested in some aspect of it. Once he has opened up, it will be easy to direct the talk toward the subject of your article.

To return to the gentleman you are interviewing about his college years:

Don't start off with a bare, general question such as, "Tell me about your days at the University." You'll get nothing. Try the indirect approach. "I believe State University beat (its rival) at football (or whatever) while you were there." Or some item from the news of his time at college. Then let him reminisce. As you warm up to each other, it's easy to guide the conversation. You'll want to know why he chose that college. If he has children, will they go to his college? This will give you a clue to his feeling for his alma mater.

Don't start taking notes at the beginning. After a time bring out a small notebook or a folded paper such as reporters use and say, "I hope you won't mind if I take a few notes." Make your notes few unless you are going to quote him on a question of fact, then get it down fully and correctly. Same for dates, names and places.

Be curious. Don't overlook what may seem like trivial items. Notice and make a mental note of how he is dressed, how he stands or sits or walks, any mannerisms he may have, his surroundings, home or office. Is he genial and outgoing, or brusque, intense or very earnest? If he's enthusiastic on some topic, remember what it is. If he shies away from a subject, try to find out why. Take down words he uses over and over and a few actual words to indicate his manner of speech and his train of thought. These are all clues to his personality and will add color to your article.

Keep him on subjects that interest him—remember that the most interesting person to anyone is himself—so you can keep the conversational ball rolling.

Get anecdotes. They will not only add spice to your piece, but give you dialogue which makes for easy reading. Ask such questions as, "What were some of the most amusing things that happened to you at college? I'm sure it wasn't all work and no play." Or, "What did you enjoy most at college? What did you like least?" Even, "Were there any student rebellions in your day?" You may lead him into a stream of reminiscences out of which may come anecdotes that will be pertinent to your piece.

Don't forget you want information, too. Ask questions such as, "What do you value most from your college education? What has meant most in your career? In your private life?" Learn what he thinks of colleges today. Was there some college experience he wouldn't want to repeat if he were a student today? Does he see some of his old college friends now? If so, whom? You may want to talk with them.

Don't do all the talking yourself. In my own early days, if there was a lull in the conversation, I would start babbling nervously. A pause may occur while your subject is thinking; wait for him. If it's one of those dry moments, take a quick look at the questions you came prepared with, and go into another subject.

Don't try to seem smarter than you are. You are not there to impress him. Acknowledge the fact that you don't know something he has mentioned or the name of a person he takes for granted you know, and ask him just who this is.

If he has agreed to give you only thirty minutes, at the end of that time make a motion to go unless he is obviously so interested that he wants you to stay longer. Sometimes a short interview will go on because the person wants to keep talking.

Before you leave, thank him for his time and try to make a date for a second appointment. When you go over your notes later, you may find omissions you need to fill in. If the interview takes place in your subject's office, stop at his secretary's desk as you go out and thank her for holding the time for you. Get her name and say you may want to call her back. Make her your friend; she can be helpful.

Get to your typewriter as soon as possible and write up your interview while it is still fresh. Put down what was said and your impressions of your interviewee. Then you should have a graphic account of the important points. Next make notes on what you want to ask him in a second interview.

You will undoubtedly want to talk with other people who know him now or who knew him when he was a student—his associates, his professors, his family, his classmates, the athletic coach, if he was active in sports.

There are two schools of thought on whether you should see these secondary people before you talk with your principal or afterward. If you see them beforehand, question them tactfully. A young writer I know had an assignment from a magazine to write a story on a well-known woman doctor. Before meeting the doctor she talked with everyone she could find who knew or had worked with the lady. Word got back to the doctor, who felt the reporter had been prying, and she closed up like a clam.

If you do secondary interviewing afterward, you can talk not only with people who admire him but with those who don't. You will want to see him from all sides. He can't be a paragon. Knowing some of his weaknesses will make it possible for you to present him as a real human being. From his friends and family you are likely to get your best anecdotes.

When you come to write your article, if you have quoted from your subject directly, it is a good idea to call him back and read the quotation to make sure that you are correct: also make a last check with him on names and dates. It is not advisable to show him the complete profile. Too often he may want to redo the whole piece.

A day or so after your last interview with the subject of

your article, write him a short note thanking him for his cooperation. This small act of courtesy is too often forgotten.

Tape recorders

Should you use a tape recorder? Some experienced writers use it successfully. I would not advise it for a beginner. In any case, find out ahead of time whether your subject agrees to it. Some people are struck dumb by this mechanical gadget. But movie stars and many public figures who are accustomed to it, prefer it; they feel sure that they will be quoted accurately. Be sure, too, that you have had experience operating a recorder and can put it into action quickly and unobtrusively.

Occasionally you will find someone who refuses to be interviewed. Then you must use your wits. I was once assigned to do a short biographical sketch of the director of a Museum of the American Indian. Before asking for an appointment, I looked up all the usual sources and could not find a line on him—finally one five-line paragraph in the library of the American Museum of Natural History. It gave his name, a few dates, and that was all. I telephoned him to ask if I might see him. Courteously but firmly he declined. "I will be glad to give you any facts you desire on the Museum, but I do not care for personal publicity." I seemed to be at a dead end until I said that I was also at work on an article on the pre-Columbian American Indian and would he read it over for facts. He agreed.

The next day I went to the Museum and gave my piece to the director—a charming man. He read the article and made some comments and corrections. When he handed it back to me, I said, "I understand that you are part Indian. What is your tribe?" When he said, "Navaho," we were off. For I had made a long study of the Navahos and was very enthusiastic about them. Soon we were chatting like old friends, and I got my little story about him.

The moral of this is, "If you find one door closed, look for another one."

Practice sessions

If all this seems like a difficult and formidable undertaking, put your mind at rest. Here are some tips on how, in your daily conversations with your own friends, you can coach yourself in the technique of asking questions:

1. Teach yourself to become a good listener. Few of us are. When an acquaintance gives us an opinion or recounts an experience, we have a tendency to jump in immediately, often before he has completed his thought, with our own opinion or a similar experience of our own. As a result we have expressed ourselves and learned nothing. Train yourself to listen attentively and sympathetically; give the speaker the feeling that you regard his opinions highly and are truly interested in his experience. Instead of grabbing the conversational ball, ask questions to lead him on. If you disagree, phrase a question such as, "But what do you think about. . . ." and cite an opposite point of view that will provoke him into a defense of his own opinion.

You will emerge with a clear image of your friend's convictions, and a greater understanding of him. And you will be training yourself for a professional interview. Incidentally, you will be making yourself popular; everyone loves a good listener.

2. Don't ask "loaded" questions which ask only for

agreement. Suppose you are discussing a nursery school teacher with a parent whose child is in the same class as yours. If you say, "Don't you think Miss X is an incompetent teacher?" you may merely get an agreement. But if you ask, "What do you think of the way Miss X handles little Jimmy Jones?" you are likely to get her unbiased opinion based on her experience with Miss X.

You may not have converted your friend to your way of thinking, but you will have learned what she really thinks. What you want from the subject of your profile is his opinion, not simply a confirmation of your own opinions and views.

3. Learn to go into an interview with an open mind. In your private life, when you are about to meet a new acquaintance—someone who seems important to you and whom you are glad to know—you look forward to the introduction with pleasure. Approach an interview in the same way. You will find this an excellent antidote for nervousness, your own good humor may be communicated to your interviewee, and you'll be off to a good start.

4. You can also train your memory. Truman Capote states that he took no notes for *In Cold Blood,* although he quotes people verbatim at great length. He says he trained himself to transcribe conversation by having a friend read aloud passages from a book for a couple of hours a day. Later he wrote the passages from memory to see how close he could come to the original. After a year and a half, he could recall with 95% accuracy. While few of us have the time or patience to keep this up for eighteen months, it is an exercise well worth trying whenever you have an obliging friend nearby and a free hour or so. A retentive memory is an endowment to be prized.

א 6

THE LEAD

SOME WRITERS WAIT until they have finished an article before writing the lead. Others say they must have a lead before they can get into the body of a piece they are working on. I know one successful free lance who says, "The lead gives me not only a starting point but it sets the mood and pace of my piece. Once I have that, I can sail right in." But getting that lead may take her two days of pacing the floor and writing one version after another. Others give themselves a day or half day to come up with a lead. If none comes by then, they go on to writing the body of the article and go back to the lead later.

Pulling power

No matter when you write your lead—last, first, or in the middle of doing your article—it is the most important paragraph in your piece. For it is here that you either hook your reader or lose him. Once you've lost him, he may be lost to you forever—as far as he is concerned, you might just as well have written the balance of your article in your diary.

Even before the article reaches the reader, a persuasive lead attracts the editor and helps along the sale.

To demonstrate to yourself the pulling power of the lead, look over your own shoulder as you leaf through a new magazine. When you turn to a new page, you glance at the title, illustration and blurb, then scan the first two or three sentences. If the writer's approach interests you, you'll read on to see what he has to say; if it doesn't, you'll turn to something else and probably never return to it.

There are as many kinds of good leads as there are good articles; but here are a dozen basic or classic forms that are popular today:

1. *The portrait lead.* This is most often used to introduce a profile or human interest piece. We have an excellent example in an article on Adam Clayton Powell:

> As a bell rang, a tall, handsome man broke off his chat with a friend and said, "Well, I'd better go in and get on the payroll." The speaker was Harlem's fashion plate firebrand, Adam Clayton Powell, Jr., 54, chairman of one of the House's most influential committees, pastor of perhaps the nation's largest Protestant church, celebrated junketeer and one of the most controversial figures in U. S. politics.

This portrait not only gives us in capsule Powell's characteristics, but points the way to those facets of his personality the author will explore. This tantalizing first glimpse sharpens our interest and we want to get on with the piece.

2. *The anecdotal lead.* This is probably the most popular lead and, if well done, is an almost sure-fire attention-getter because everybody loves a story. Leaf through any issue of any popular magazine to discover how surely the anecdote draws you into the article. Here is one I especially like because it has a little surprise at the end. It is from *Good Housekeeping* (March, 1966) and opens an article entitled "Some of the Nicest People Are Superstitious" by Winifred Wolfe:

> One woman who married a Texan over thirty-one years ago refuses to let him replace the tiny chip in her engagement ring with a bigger diamond. He certainly can afford it now, but the lady is stubborn. When she says, "Lyndon, I don't want another diamond; I like this one," she means it.

This may seem like a far-fetched opening for an article on superstitions. But the author ties it in with her next paragraph:

> Sentiment or superstition? Dr. George Chalpin, a noted Boston psychiatrist, claims the two are so closely allied that it's almost impossible to tell where one begins and the other ends. Like Mrs. LBJ, most women feel. . . .

In writing the anecdotal lead, pick out the most dramatic or appropriate incident you have gathered in your research and tell it in a straightforward manner.

Another example:

> Last spring a thirty-year-old housewife, whom we shall call Alice Adams, looked up from the sleeping baby in her arms and found the room swimming around her. "That's

odd," she thought. When she tried to rise to put the baby down, she found herself too dizzy to get to her feet and wave after wave of nausea swept over her. Terrified, she edged the chair to the crib, got the baby safely inside and crawled to the telephone. "Tell Dr. Allen to please come right away," she said. "I'm terribly dizzy and sick. I think I must be having a stroke."

This might introduce an article on an inner ear disorder.

It goes without saying that an anecdote concerning the President's wife or any person in public life should be factually true; the same rule holds for anyone who is identified by name and residence. The anecdote concerning the "thirty-year-old housewife whom we will call Alice Adams" need not have happened exactly as told since she is not identified, but something very similar could have happened. The writer's medical research had shown that inner ear trouble occurs at any age, and it was more dramatic when ascribed to a young mother with her baby than it would have been to a grandmother with her knitting. The spirit of truth is there.

3. *The shocker.* The aim of this lead is to shake the reader by some dramatic statement and so capture his interest. Here are three examples:

a) "More divorced men die between forty-five and fifty-four than single, widowed or married men of the same age."

b) "Your eight-year-old today may know more mathematics than you did when you entered college."

c) "Every five minutes some American meets his death

by accident; every three seconds someone is injured. How many of these could have been prevented?"

Or this from "We Ask the Wrong Questions About Crime" by William M. McCord from *The New York Times Magazine* (November 21, 1965):

America is by far the most criminal nation in the world. On a per capita basis, Americans commit about twice as many assaults as Frenchmen, triple the number of rapes as Italians, and five times as many murders as Englishmen.

When you make a positive declaration of this kind, be sure that your statement is correct. Do not depend on hearsay or on a piece in another popular magazine. Go to the source: Public Health Reports, National Safety Council, U. S. Office of Education, Federal Bureau of Investigation—to name a few. An excellent source for statistics is the *World Almanac* or the *Information Please Almanac*. Both give the original sources for their statistics.

4. *The self-interest lead* answers the reader's question of "What's in it for me?" It invites him to read on to discover what you are going to tell him that will benefit him or his family, even his community. Here are some examples:

A suburban housewife, bored after the last of her children were well along in school, has begun a new life for herself. She has just enrolled for a course in archeology at What's-It University. She says as soon as her youngest is in college, she's going to join a "dig."

The reader may think she could find something equally interesting.

Another:

A little girl, waiting in front of her New Jersey home for her mother to back the car out the drive and pick her up, was stabbed by a man who made a quick get-away; the child died on the way to the hospital. A twelve-year-old boy, looking after his little brother in a play area of New York's Central Park, was stabbed by a band of teen-agers. An eight-year-old boy, trying out his birthday bicycle on Boston's Esplanade, was momentarily out of the sight of his waiting father. He trudged back a few minutes later, dirty, bloody and with a broken collarbone. Two older boys had thrown him to the ground and made off with his bike.

These are not neglected children. Is there any way a parent can protect them?

The reader's thought is, "They could have been my own."

Finally the classic and sure-fire opening for a reducing article: "Would you like to eat what you like and still keep a slim figure?" If you are going to give advice on dieting, be sure you have a reputable authority behind you.

5. *The straight declarative lead* is effective in special interest magazines or when the subject has a wide appeal. For example:

a) About twelve years ago a small manufacturer started on an experiment for which women have called him blessed. He was looking for a process which would keep pleats crisp without ironing.

b) Almost every parent would like to have his boy go to

college; now the Anti-Poverty Program brings college within the reach even of students from low-income families.

This excellent one is from *Redbook* (November, 1963):

c) John Kennedy, one of the two men alive who literally have the power to destroy the human race, believes that American women can play an important part in preventing such destruction.

6. *The first-person lead* finds its home most often in the personal experience article:

I had always promised myself I would never be a nagging wife. And I think I kept that promise until Jim had his first heart attack and the doctor said, "Cut down on smoking, cut down on cocktails, cut down on rich foods." I didn't realize I was nagging every time I reminded him, "Don't you think you've had enough, dear?" until one day. . . .

This lead is also useful if you are ghostwriting a piece for a celebrity, where the first person promises a glimpse behind the scenes with your VIP. Reminiscences are in the first person throughout.

7. *The action lead* plunges right into the middle of the scene and promises more excitement to come:

The police dispatcher's voice rasped over the intercom: "195 South Street. Two-car crack up. Some injured. Maybe dead." Within minutes a police car pushed through the crowd. The woman pinned down by the wreck was screaming. . . .

This pinpoints the moment of crisis. It is effective in articles of adventure, of sports (the goal that wins or loses the game), or of disaster or of hard-won accomplishment.

8. *The informative* or *let's-get-up-to-date lead.* This is effective when the subject is sure-fire (a new health discovery) or controversial; or the article is written for a publication whose readers are devotees of its theme. The lead tells the reader that you are going to give him the latest information on a subject. For example:

Have our cities rushed into the fluoridation of the water supply without enough study? Are the good effects of the fluorides on children's teeth sufficient to outweigh the possible ill effect of a buildup of this enzyme in kidneys, heart, liver and lungs? Have we a right to impose mass medication on diverse and vulnerable human beings?

I wanted to know. I have collected opinions from the eminent authorities in both camps. Here are their answers.

9. *The news lead* ties the article in with a subject that is in the news. Here is one from "Dating by Computer" produced by Gene Shalit for *Look* (February 22, 1966):

"How come you're still single? Don't you know any nice computers?"

Perhaps no mother has yet said that to her daughter, but don't bet it won't happen, because Big Matchmaker is watching you. From Boston to Berkeley, computer dates are sweeping the campus, replacing old-fashioned boy-meets-girl devices; punch bowls are out, punch cards are in.

10. *The philosophical lead* finds a place when it reveals

the inner thought of the person portrayed rather than his external traits:

a) Whatever our religion, we are all pagan followers of Pan when the daffodils dance in the warm spring sun.
b) When Sister William Mary bid me goodbye with her, "And may God be with you," she left with me some of her own serene and happy spirit.

Be sure to follow such a lead with ideas that are really worthwhile. Don't hand the reader trite maxims.

11. *The if-only lead* is sometimes called the *paradoxical lead*. The author states a negative opinion and then goes into his positive article by the back door, so to speak. It is effective when well done, but it must be exactly right, for the article and the transition to the body of the piece must be simple and explicit.

If Big Joe Arnold, when he limped back to Breathitt County, Kentucky, after Appomattox, had thought that one day his great-grandson would go down to the Bluegrass for book larnin', he would. . . .

12. *The humorous lead* is excellent if you have a really amusing anecdote that will be acceptable to your readers; otherwise it can be as dull as a toastmaster's trite introduction. This is hard to work out just right, so drop it if it doesn't come off.

The source of leads

Just as illustrators clip magazines for pictures of fashions, places and people for reference later in their drawings, so some writers, when they find a lead that appeals, clip it and put it in a folder. If at some point they are stuck for a lead, they leaf through the collection, not to copy, but to put their own thinking on a fresh track.

Your lead may grow out of your own article. But make it brief. If you find yourself wound up in words, or if your idea requires a long explanation, try another approach. It should give your reader a vivid impression, and it should reach out toward him. For these qualities you might well turn to fiction to see how the storytellers and novelists begin. Here are three of my favorites:

From Tolstoy's *Anna Karenina*: "Happy families are all alike. Every unhappy family is unhappy in its own way."

From Sinclair Lewis's *Elmer Gantry*: "Elmer Gantry was drunk. He was eloquently drunk, lovingly and pugnaciously drunk. He leaned against the bar of the Old Home Sample Room, the most gilded and urbane saloon in Cato, Missouri, and requested the bartender to join him in 'The Good Old Summer Time', the waltz of the day."

From Jane Austen's *Pride and Prejudice*: "It is a truth universally acknowledged that a single man in possession of a good fortune must be in want of a wife."

Arlene Silberman, a writer with a passion for perfection, writes and rewrites indefatigably. In an article which she was then calling "The Orphans of the Living", the lead had reached this version on her sixth revision:

Call her Betsy or Mary or Jane. Call him Timmy or Tommy or Ted. The name doesn't matter. What *does* matter is that they are foster children—a few of the 280,000 youngsters in the United States today who have neither mother nor father to care for them. Many have been bounced from foster homes to institutions and back again ever since they were born out of wedlock, or their father deserted, or their neighbors complained that the children were being abused or neglected. Only a small handful are orphans. But 125,000 more are orphans of the living. They will neither return home nor be adopted. Instead, they will live out their childhood in No Man's Land.

Take Jimmy, a freckle-faced nine-year-old with a cowlick in back and two big teeth in front. He has known six homes in four years. Small wonder he was bewildered when the coach of the Little League team said, "I don't think we've met before. Whose boy are you?"

Jimmy's doleful answer tells the story. "I'm nobody's nothin'."

After many other tries, Mrs. Silberman found her final lead. The article appeared in *Good Housekeeping* (September, 1964), under the title "Must These Children Live Without Love?" This is the opening:

"And whose little sweetheart are *you?*" the department-store Santa asked the five-year-old girl who had just climbed into his ample lap. Most of his small customers were only too eager to tell him—and make sure he got the spelling straight. But this little girl stopped him in his tracks.

"I'm nobody's nothin'," she said quietly. Santa had come upon a child in foster care.

The improvement here is obvious. The final lead is shorter, more poignant and engages the reader immediately. It is focused on one child, rather than on a number, and the statistic—280,000 foster children in the United States—comes later in the body of the article.

This is another example of the anecdote that need not be literally factual. In the earlier version the child was

Jimmy and the questioner the Little League coach; in the final version it was Dolores and the department-store Santa. The actual participants may have been a Sammy and his school teacher. As it happens, the author was relating an actual response from a foster child, but was changing the setting in which it occurred. Even if she had invented the anecdote, however, the spirit of truth would still be there because it is the sort of thing that could have happened.

Titles

This example leads to another thought I would like to leave with you. Don't work too hard on your title. Do give your piece a title when you submit it, and if you have one you think is especially good, by all means use it. But don't be upset if the editor rewrites it. He does that in eight cases out of ten. He may do it because, coming to the piece fresh, he sees a compelling angle that you might have overlooked. Sometimes he rewrites to make it conform to the theme of his own publication; and sometimes a longer or shorter title will fit in better with the art director's design for the page.

Usually the new title is an improvement. If you think it is not and you know of the change in advance (often the editor may not even tell you), you can make a mild protest. But if he likes his own better, just grin and bear it.

7

THE ANECDOTE

ONE OF THE most important items in any writer's bag of skills is the ability to use anecdotes effectively. Where do you find them? You look for them. When you are doing the research and interviewing for your article, you keep a wary eye out for the little story or incident that will add color to your piece. As you scan the articles in the magazines on your reading table, you will discover that professional writers use the anecdote for many purposes.

Why, when, where

An anecdote is one of the sure-fire ways *to begin an article*. Here its purpose is to capture the interest of the reader and persuade him to read on.

It has an important place in *the body of the article* to introduce another topic in your argument, to act as a transition from one topic to another, to illustrate a point you are making and to keep the reader's interest alive.

As *the conclusion of your piece,* an anecdote can top off your subject, sometimes summarize it, and leave the reader with your own final opinion. At the end of a profile, it can reveal your hero as courageous, sympathetic, amusing or (if your piece is critical), as careless, erratic or whatever; or as a combination of both good and bad qualities.

Writing effective anecdotes calls for the ability to tell a good story. But you have heard many a good story slaughtered in the telling: a speaker at least has his voice, facial expressions, and gestures to help him make his point, but the writer has none of these and must rely on his ability with words.

We will define the anecdote here as any short, pointed story or incident or human-interest item. If it is a story, it should have a beginning, middle, and end, even if it runs only a few lines. In any case, it must be relevant to the purpose of your article. Don't throw in even a good story unless it advances the point you want to prove in your article. Don't put it in just because it happened.

The anecdote at the beginning of an article. Here is a telling anecdote which was used by Dixie Dean Trainer, one of my students who has become a successful contributor to many magazines. She used it to open a profile of Madame Helena Rubenstein entitled, "Tiniest Tycoon," in *Coronet* (February, 1964):

> She is so tiny that, when traveling, she props her feet on a small cosmetic case—which contains a quarter of a million dollars worth of jewelry. She also takes her lunch to work in a brown paper bag and her favorite words are "too much." A former associate once remarked, "If somebody offered

Rubenstein a package of chewing gum for a nickel, she would say 'too much' in the hope that it was the only package of gum in the world that could be bought for four cents."

The author has in not much more than one hundred words given us a graphic introduction to the lady with emphasis on her thrift, as well as her wealth. Having thus aroused the reader's interest, she goes into the main body of her story. The next sentence is, "Her name is Helena Rubenstein, and she is the richest self-made woman in the world." After that start, Madame Rubenstein's life story follows naturally.

Often writers begin with several short incidents that emphasize the theme of the article and prove that a problem is widespread. Paul W. Kearney used this device in "How to Lick the Hazards of Foul Weather Driving," an article published in *Family Safety* (Winter, 1963, National Safety Council) and condensed in *Reader's Digest* (December, 1963), with the following opening:

"All of a sudden I saw two or three cars spread across the road. I hit my brakes but couldn't stop and ran into one car. Then another car hit me from behind, and another hit that one."

This, from a bed in Perth Amboy, N. J., General Hospital, was a victim's play-by-play description of a type of accident that is becoming increasingly common: the multiple car pile-up.

On that foggy day, this victim was one of 28 injured in a series of crack-ups involving 59 cars on New Jersey's Garden State Parkway.

On the Santa Ana Freeway last fall 11 persons were injured when 40 cars piled up in one grand melee. Near Ocean-side, Calif., seven were killed and four critically injured in a five-car crash during a blinding rain storm. On the New Jersey Turnpike a 16-car episode in the fog injured five. Next day a 17-car chain reaction in the fog on the same turnpike killed two and injured 13.

In this case, if the writer had stopped with his first anecdote, the reader might have thought this an isolated accident. By adding the other incidents, he piled up his evidence and showed that such disasters are nationwide. His next sentence is, "Why these pile-ups?" The article answers the question and suggests remedies.

Anecdotes in the body of the article: Let me illustrate this by a description of an article I once wrote on the services a family counseling agency renders to people in trouble. I opened with what seemed to me my most dramatic anecdote, the story of a marriage about to break up and how the counselors at the agency saved it. The article goes on to say that this is only one of the family difficulties the agency tries to solve: the man of fifty who has lost his job, the pregnant unmarried girl, the teen-age dropout and others. To illustrate each problem there was a short case history of such a person in trouble. These anecdotes moved the article along and helped the reader to identify with the problem. I collected them as I interviewed family counselors in various states. And for some I drew on my personal experience.

The anecdote as a conclusion to the article: As an illustration of the anecdote that winds up a piece, we return to the article on Madame Rubenstein. After the story-telling opening, the author tells of Madame's various adventures in business and in her private life, with emphasis on her love for making money and her unbounded energy for work. This is the conclusion:

> But there is evidence, somewhat touching, that her slavish devotion to work springs from something deeper than simply a desire to make ever so much money. When she was asked why she didn't slow down, she replied in shocked tones, "Why, what would happen to all my people if I gave up? I feel I have to work all the time harder. My people, they want leisure, much more than I."

This gentle ending not only gives the underlying reason for much that the writer has recounted, but leaves the reader in a sympathetic mood toward that remarkable woman.

Revealing incidents that have the effect of an anecdote: Often colorful facts or homely—almost trivial—incidents or specific and carefully observed details serve to portray the underlying character of a person. One such I remember vividly. *McCall's* had commissioned a writer to do a piece on the home life of Mrs. Eleanor Roosevelt in the Hyde Park cottage where she lived after the President's death.

With Mrs. Roosevelt's permission, the writer visited the cottage and followed the housekeeper at her various tasks which, that day, included putting away the freshly ironed laundry. Almost every one of the fine old damask table cloths, the writer reported, wore a careful darn or patch. Mrs. Roosevelt's personal clothes were simply laid out on her bed. The lady of the house preferred to put them away herself. Our author learned, too, that Mrs. Roosevelt's favorite dessert was Jell-o.

I have forgotten much else about the article, but these small details remain with me as a picture of the simplicity and love of home of the "First Lady of the World." They also indicate how her Victorian upbringing had carried over into the last decade of her life.

Details

This meticulous observation of detail—and inclusion of it in a manuscript—is one of the marks of the professional magazine writer. It is one of the skills that many newspaper reporters who aspire to magazine writing often lack and have difficulty learning. The reporter has been trained to gather facts, and he gives them to you straight. The magazine writer is also sure of his facts, but he presents them with color and insight, and he writes in specifics, not generalities.

The reporter might write, for example, "The drive to the house is lined with trees." The magazine writer would say, "The quarter-mile drive to the red brick house is lined with tall locusts in bloom," or "with moss-hung live oaks" or "with sycamores that meet in an arch at the top," or whatever. In other words, he leaves you with a picture. Where the reporter tells that someone served "a typical Southern dinner," the magazine writer would say, "She served crisp fried chicken with milk gravy and watermelon pickles and little light biscuits."

The articles editor of a national women's magazine, recounting her troubles in getting an acceptable piece from a Washington reporter, said, "All I get from her are bare bones. She describes a White House luncheon table by saying that it was set with fine china, linen and silver. But try to get her to tell what every woman wants to know: that the cloth was lace, if that is true, that the china was Lenox in the grape pattern, the silver early Williamsburg and the glasses French crystal; that the table appointments had been selected by the current First Lady, or one of her predecessors, and which one."

Statistics

When you are dealing in statistics, the use of specifics rather than generalities can serve to keep your reader awake. If you write that a proposed increase in school taxes would add half a million dollars to the city's annual revenue, you will leave your reader nodding. But if you write that the mayor or school superintendent (or whoever your authority is) says that the increase would pay for the much needed High School in the Buena Vista suburb, or would provide hot school lunches for every child in town, you have given the reader something definite to think about and you have appealed to his self-interest.

Now for a word of caution. Don't interrupt your anecdote with stray facts and bits of information that should have gone either before or after it. These only slow up the story and distract the reader. To illustrate what not to do, I'm paraphrasing the lead to a manuscript I recently read. The article concerns a country doctor in a backwoods community:

> The telephone in Dr. William Reese's office rang insistently. It was seven P.M. of a snowy winter's day, and the doctor had been on the go since six in the morning. (He had been about to leave for home.) He took down the receiver wearily. "It's Miz Calhoun up on Fox Hollow, Doc Bill."

(They called him Doc Bill in that community. Fox Hollow was five miles out a dirt road.) "Ole man Colby's boy just come down the hill. He says his maw's took bad. Wants you right away. The baby's comin'."

"Ask the boy how long his mother has been in pain." (He hears her repeat the question.)

"He says she's been takin' on terrible a long time."

"Tell him to go back and have his mother stay in bed. Tell his father to put a wash boiler of clean water on the stove to heat. I'll be there soon as I can make it."

The doctor buckled on his galoshes. (He'd told Colby a year ago that his wife shouldn't have any more babies, but they didn't practice birth control out there.) He shrugged into his fleece-lined coat and reached for his obstetric kit. (A midwife usually helped on these cases, but she was laid up with the flu.)

As he opened the door he was met by an icy blast. (It had been snowing all day, now sleeting.) The roads were a sheet of ice. (These roads were poor at any time.) The jeep started. (As he backed out into the road, he looked at the plot of ground where he hoped some day to have a hospital. He'd been trying to raise the money for it for almost two years now.) He made it to the crossroads and slid into a snow bank. Later, a pulpwood truck gave him a shove. Then up into the hills. At the turnoff, he left the jeep and took the last mile on foot. Three steps forward and two back. Finally the dim light of the Colby cabin. He had reached the suffering woman in time. (The other five little Colbys were sleeping on a pallet in a corner.)

Six hours later the baby was born. The mother would live. Fox Hollow had a new citizen and old man Colby another mouth to feed.

When Dr. Reese left the cabin, dawn was breaking. He had had a 24-hour day and another was beginning.

Now re-read this, skipping all the sentences in parentheses and you will find a taut anecdote that introduces the doctor, shows the hardships he faces and presents him as a devoted physician. The parenthetical sentences belong elsewhere in the article.

To show you a well-constructed anecdote, here is the beginning of an article by Alice Lake which appeared in *McCall's* (December, 1964). The article is entitled "Five Came to Aberdeen."

By 12:15 P.M. the X-rays were dry. Dr. Paul R. Leon, one of two radiologists in Aberdeen, South Dakota, called Dr. James N. Berbos, who had just started office hours at the Aberdeen Medical Center, three blocks from the hospital. "On the Fischer X-rays," he said, "there are five babies, doctor."

Half listening, a patient already on the examining table, Dr. Berbos asked, "How many?"

"Five, doctor."

"How many?"

"Five. How many times have you delivered five babies."

"Well, never."

"Well, I've never had five on one X-ray."

Did it really happen?

Your next question might be, "Does an anecdote have to be written just exactly as it happened?" The answer is, "not always."

If you are quoting an actual person, you should stick pretty closely to his own words. Even there, since conversations tend to be prosy and filled with "ers" and "ums," you may well sharpen your story by omitting irrelevant phrases. Just make sure that by cutting you have not mis-quoted your subject.

If, however, you are employing an anecdote merely to bring home a point, you have more leeway. Let me illus-trate:

One day some years ago I met an old friend on a bus. Her little boy Jimmy had been unhappy in school and when I inquired how he was getting along, she said, "He's the most unpopular child in his class. He can't seem to learn to play with other children—they tease him. Every afternoon when he comes home, I think I can't stand it if he's had another hard day. I find myself praying that things have for once gone well with him."

Such an incident might inspire you to write an article on the unpopular child. First, you would talk with teachers and child psychologists to learn the best way for a parent to handle such a child. Your anecdote might go something like this:

> Mrs. Ellison stood at her living room window, looking across her neighbor's lawn down the street. Behind her the grandfather clock on the stair sounded the half hour—half-past three—and as if on signal the school bus stopped at the corner. "Oh, dear God," she prayed, her fingers laced tightly together, "let this have been a good day. Don't let him have had another bad time."

The purpose of this anecdote was simply to show the anguish a person suffers over the unhappiness of a loved one. You could have adapted it to a wife whose out-of-work husband is returning from an interview about a job he hoped to get; or to a parent whose son might have muffed his college entrance exams. All that is necessary in such a case is that the incident be believable and could have happened to the person you are writing about.

This ability to recount an incident or to tell a short story well is one of the skills that today's writer of narrative articles can borrow from fiction. Occasionally, an anecdote based on fact can be expanded into a short article. Try some of O. Henry's short stories for a pattern.

ℵ 8

DIALOGUE

IF YOU HAVE ever watched a child selecting books for his own reading, you may have seen him discard one with the statement, "I don't want this book. There's no talking in it." The adult reader would probably not be so plainspoken, but he also is attracted by a page in which the text is broken by dialogue or direct quotes. It makes for easy reading and promises human interest.

Words and rhythms of fiction

It goes without saying that the ability to write convincing dialogue is an imperative for the writer of fiction. He uses dialogue to reveal characteristics of the person he is portraying; to move his story forward; often to establish time and place; even to indicate the background and social standing of his hero.

Dialogue and quotes have an important place also in today's narrative article and for much the same reasons. Since our great novelists and short story writers have mastered the technique of letting a character speak for himself, the non-fiction writer will do well to turn to fiction for guidance. As a first step read fictional dialogue, analyze it to discover what makes it effective, and apply what you have learned to your own work.

As you read, observe how written speech changes with changing times. Compare, for instance, the dialogue in one of Dickens' novels with that of a Hemingway short story. At one point in *David Copperfield* when Miss Trotwood is arranging for David to stay with Mr. Wickford and is embarrassed to mention price, Mr. Wickford reassures her: "Come! I know what you mean. . . . You shall not be oppressed by the receipt of favors, Miss Trotwood. You may pay for him if you like."

The sentence, "You shall not be oppressed by the receipt of favors," speaks of a time when manners had grace and dignity and the reader had leisure to enjoy rolling phrases.

Now turn to one of Hemingway's short stories. Here the dialogue is fast, often staccato, and the choice of words is casual. Life moves at a faster pace and speech reflects the times.

As a non-fiction writer you will not employ dialogue as lavishly as a storyteller does, but if you use it well and catch the words and rhythms of your speaker, you will give a professional flavor to your piece. Poorly written dialogue is the mark of an amateur.

Means and ends

With this preface, let's get down to the hows and whys of dialogue in the article, its purpose and what it accomplishes.

1. Dialogue or direct quotes may introduce a character and indicate the sort of person he is. An effective example is seen in the opening paragraph (which we have looked at earlier) of a profile of Adam Clayton Powell by Ernest Dunbar in *Look* (May 7, 1963). It reads:

> Shortly after noon on a cold, blustery day last January, members of the newly elected Congress were assembled in the Chamber of the House of Representatives, waiting to take their oath of office. As a bell rang, a tall, handsome man broke off his chat with a friend and said, "Well, I'd better go in and get on the payroll."

The short quote, "Well, I'd better go in and get on the payroll," gives the reader a quick picture of Powell's attitude toward his job. Notice how the combination of narrative and quote permits the scene, the character and his method of speaking all to be introduced rapidly and simultaneously.

Another example is Robert Deardorff's article, "Ringo Starr: Domesticated Beatle" (*Redbook,* September, 1965). Ringo is talking about his youth:

> In those days the family never had much money. "We're working-class people," he pointed out. "My mother worked all her life—as long as I can remember. She was a bar maid first. Then she worked in a shop selling fruit. Besides that, she had to keep an eye on me, you know, and take care of herself and the house. But we had a nice home—for what we had, you know. We didn't ever live in squalor."

He remembered, too, that he had always had "the best

my mother could give me. . . . She was just great, you know."

The quote shows that he was not ashamed of his poverty-harassed youth, that he had a deep love for his mother, and he comes through as a gentle, sensitive young man. It is his own words that carry conviction.

2. Quotes alone can make up an anecdote, as in the following often-told story of Lady Astor and Winston Churchill:

"If you were my husband, I'd poison your coffee," Lady Astor said in one famous exchange. "If you were my wife, I'd drink it," replied Churchill.

3. Dialogue can define and give the color of a place. Often a few sentences straight from the mouth of a person tell more about where he comes from than a page of description. The man from Maine, for instance, does not use the same expressions as the citizen of Mississippi. The Bostonian's turn of phrase is not the same as the Texan's. Reporters who have quoted Presidents Kennedy and Johnson have been adept in capturing the differences in their intonations and use of words.

This brings us back to that basic qualification of a writer—a good ear. If you don't have it, cultivate it. Listen to what you hear. Be on the lookout for those special intonations, turns of expression, cadences, phrases and words that are characteristic of each individual. Then you will be able to write speech which *reads* as people speak it. As you come across revealing phrases, put them down in your notebook so they will be on tap when you need them.

In one of my own notebooks, I find an account of a visit I made one autumn to a fox hound meet in South Carolina. I was following the hunt with a local hunter who suggested that we wait in a certain place for the hounds to come through. "If'n we make a lose on this side," he said, "we'll get 'um on the other." He described one of his own hounds as having "a big squalling mouth." Both "make a lose" and "big squalling mouth" are colorful, regional expressions. I should have forgotten them if I had not put them down on the spot. Some day I'll make use of them.

A caution here on dialect. Use it sparingly. Few readers will wade through pages of heavy dialect. Write just enough at the beginning of your quotation to suggest the dialect, then go into straight prose. If you are quoting a person who habitually drops his g's, drop the final g the first few times you use it, but restore it as you go on.

4. Dialogue or direct quotes will serve to break up a long factual statement. This is a favorite device of medical and popular science writers as illustrated in an article entitled, "Diets. Why they fail and how to make them work," from *Coronet* (October, 1965). After a narrative discussion of the hazards and causes of overweight, the author says:

The American way of life is probably really to blame for the overweight of the United States population today, according to Dr. Jean Mayer of the Department of Nutrition at the Harvard School of Public Health. He writes: "The general abundance of food at a time when physical labor has become generally unnecessary, and physical exercise difficult to practice, may be responsible for much of the obesity we see."

Here the direct quote does more than break the text; by citing a well-known authority, it gives authenticity to the article. The writer establishes the status of Dr. Mayer as nutritionist by identifying him with the Department of Nutrition at the Harvard School of Public Health.

5. Direct quotes in the form of a short autobiographical statement may reveal the influences that have brought a person to his present way of thinking. A self-made man who had worked his own way through college and is now endowing college scholarships might say: "My father never went to college, and I remember his struggle to make a living. I decided, when I was ten years old, that this wouldn't happen to me. Now I want every child in the country to have a chance for a good education." The philanthropist's own words are stronger than the same information presented as third-person narrative: He remembers his father's struggle to make a living without schooling and wants American children to have a better chance.

6. Direct quotes will back up a writer's observation. Don't write, "The young man spoke wittily," and let it go at that. Let him speak for himself by giving examples of his witty remarks.

Warnings

Don't be afraid of the simple "he said." There was a time when writers strove for variety with "he quipped," "philosophized," "claimed," "observed," or with phrases such as, " 'No,' he hissed," or " 'When,' she asked tearfully." These locutions are frowned upon today.

Another caution: Although an anecdote which includes direct quotes is a popular way to begin an article, most professional writers do not start right in with the quote. When dialogue stands alone at the opening of an article, it reads as if your characters were talking in a vacuum. You will be on much surer ground if you set the stage first. Let the reader know the place, the time and the person speaking, then add the quote. Read again the first paragraph of the Adam Clayton Powell profile to see how smoothly the narrative sentences lead to the quote and then into the body of the article. If the writer had opened with "Well, I'd better go in and get on the payroll," he would have found himself in the awkward position of explaining where, who and when afterwards.

For all of its attractiveness when set on the page as such, dialogue is, nonetheless, often more effective when summarized in narrative form than when quoted directly. This is especially true when you are dealing with a professional man whose speech is full of scientific jargon that may be over the heads of your readers.

A piece describing a new scientific discovery, if written in direct quotes might read as follows: "This new discovery is going to revolutionize space travel," said Dr. Kilowatt. "The sound waves have a deep penetration and will activate. . . ." It continues in direct quotes as the scientist explains the discovery in his own technical fashion.

This would have been better if it read: "This new discovery is going to revolutionize space travel," said Dr. Kilowatt. He elaborated by describing the effect of sound waves, etc.

The narrative permits the author to translate the scientist's technical language into simple terms easily understood by the reader. At the same time, page after page in which the person quoted goes on and on in his own words can become just as tiresome to the reader as pages of unrelieved narrative prose.

A young writer just returned from Israel recently brought me a manuscript for criticism. He had interviewed an Arab citizen of Israel who felt that the Israelis were discriminating against Arabs. After a short introduction, the article was an almost literal report—one long quote after another—of what the Arab had said. The piece was long, the style became monotonous and halfway through I had lost interest. When I suggested to the author that he would have done better to tell most of the story in narrative, he replied, "But this is exactly what he said."

I pointed out that "exactly what he said," when set down on the printed page in long paragraphs rarely makes interesting reading. The speaker fumbles for words, repeats himself, starts over again. Face to face with the speaker, the interviewer will sort out the meaning, often instinctively as he listens, but the reader is unwilling to wade through the stops and starts and may give up. It is up to the writer to simplify this wordy conversation and get to the point. Often a few sentences of narration can give the sense of the argument more clearly than long paragraphs of quotes.

The author rewrote the article largely as a narrative and thus was able to share his own on-the-spot observations with the reader, to describe the setting—a poor village on the edge of the desert—and the conditions under which the Arab was living. He used quotes liberally for emphasis and to allow the Arab to speak for himself. Incidentally, he was able to reduce the length of the manuscript by one-third.

There are no hard and fast rules for narrative versus dialogue, but you might keep this in mind: When a long stretch of narration seems dull and prosy, dialogue or direct quotes—if they are pertinent to the article—will provide a change of pace. By the same token, if a series of quotes becomes dull, discursive and too long, try writing it as narrative.

Select and simplify

Dialogue, whether in fiction or non-fiction, is rarely a direct transcript of what people say in conversation. Conversation is likely to be wordy, repetitive, full of irrelevancies. It can run on forever and serve only to obscure the point at issue. To illustrate:

You are collecting material for an article on the woman executive and are interviewing executives and their co-workers in various fields—banking, politics, business, social work, etc. One of your subjects is Mrs. B, the editor of a fashion magazine. To round out your picture of her, you have asked her secretary to lunch. You have opened the conversation with, "You must find it exciting to work so closely with such a successful editor as Mrs. B. You must learn a great deal." A tape recording of what followed might run as follows:

"So that's what you think. I've got news for you. I thought that too when I took this job. I could see myself working in a nice office. It is a pretty office. It ought to be, that big decorating firm did it. All in French provincial. I'll get to be an editor myself, that's what I thought. The agency told me it would get me ahead. A stepping-stone, that's what they called it. You know the employment agency—I usually just have a tuna sandwich for lunch, sent in, but I think I'll have the chicken pie today—I don't have to watch my weight the way she does. She's on one of those new diets so she can wear a size 10. She loves to have people tell her how young she looks. Young—she'll never see fifty again. This is a nice restaurant. I've never been here before—lots of our editors eat here. That employment agency charged me a pretty fee for this job. I've got to stay till I get them paid off. That's our fiction editor over there at the corner table. She's taking an author to lunch. The company will pay for it. You know, expense account—The service *is* slow here, isn't it—I've got to go over to Seventh Avenue this afternoon. She's making a speech tomorrow. I've got to take a blue dress back and exchange it for a red one. She always wears a bright color when she's at the speakers' table. Gets more attention. Our writers have been working two days writing that speech for her. Took me till nine o'clock last night copying it—triple spaced. Now she doesn't like it. They're changing it again. Goodness knows when I'll get home tonight—I've got a date too. You'd never guess all the things she asks me to do. I took journalism in college. A lot of good that does me. I'm just a lady's maid and an errand girl. Call her husband to remind him to come home early—they're having guests. Call the housekeeper and tell her not to give little Bobby another lamb chop for lunch. Go over to Tiffany's and get her watch repaired. Then she calls me in at closing time and dictates. She'll want the letters mailed tonight. If you're a good secretary you'll never get a chance at anything else. They just keep you at it. Dessert? I'll have the vanilla ice cream with chocolate sauce.

She's at the hairdresser's now getting a touch-up. I can take
a little longer—"

And on and on.

What you will select out of all this will depend on the
slant of your article. If you are pressed for space, you might
boil it down to something like this:

> Some women executives are charged with using their
> office and staff to serve them in their personal and social
> affairs. Some are said to be inconsiderate of the people
> who work under them. The disgruntled secretary of one
> executive said:
>
> "My boss expects her secretary to be a combination of
> lady's maid and Gal Friday. I spend most of my day making
> social appointments for her and running around town on
> her personal errands. Then she calls me in at five o'clock to
> dictate and expects me to get the mail answered and posted
> before I leave. I don't get away until all hours."

We seldom write dialogue as it is spoken. We simplify
it; we rearrange it to focus on the subject; we select only
what will move the story along.

On the other hand, if you oversimplify you may lose
the personality of the speaker. For instance, in the case of
your conversation with the secretary, if your article had
been entitled "What Their Secretaries Think of Women
Executives," your purpose would have been to give the
reader a picture of the secretary, and you would have
selected different quotes. Then some of the repetitions
and unfinished sentences, even some of the irrelevancies
would have served to show the kind of person your talker

is. The writer's problem is one of selection and logical organization.

In any case, dialogue or quotes should be true to the speaker's personality. They should capture his own way with the language, the little catch phrases he tends to repeat, and his mannerisms of speech. Close observation and your own attentive ear will guide you.

If you are writing about a person you have not heard speak or about a region you are not familiar with, better stick to narrative.

ℵ 9

HOW TO BRING PEOPLE TO LIFE

"WHAT'S HE LIKE?"

That is the first question we ask of anyone who is reporting on a meeting with a person whose life promises to touch on our own. It is also asked by the reader of any writer, whether of fiction or non-fiction, who is introducing to us a person, imaginary or real.

Imagine for a moment that you are a newly engaged girl and have just come home from meeting your future mother-in-law. Here are some of the questions with which your waiting family will greet you:

What does she look like?

What kind of person is she?

What did she say?

How does she act?

Do other people like her?

And finally, Do you like her?

If you are writing a comprehensive profile, you will probably answer a similar list of questions, for your entire article is devoted to building up, block by block, your impression of your subject; or, at least that facet or that part of his life you wish to portray. Even in introducing a subsidiary character, you will do well to answer some of these questions for yourself. In any case, you should know the answers to all of them whether or not you make use of the complete list.

What does he look like?

Since it is physical appearance we first observe on meeting a new person, most writers get in a description of his looks early in the article. This gives the reader the first clue to the kind of person he is. If he is tall and brawny and walks with assurance, he may be considered capable. If he is skinny and hesitant, one is prepared to find him irresolute. How is he dressed? If he is well-tailored and meticulous, he may be expected to be methodical and fastidious. If he is carelessly dressed, not too clean, with bushy hair and beard, "another youth in revolt" may be the verdict.

A revealing picture of a person's appearance, which also gives a clue to his personality, may often be achieved in a few words. Here are half a dozen brief and graphic portraits by master writers and an excellent class exercise by a student:

In a chapter titled "Will Strunk," from his book *The Points of My Compass* (Harper & Row), E. B. White describes the professor who had taught him the elements of style at Cornell:

> From every line [of his 'little book'] there peers out at me the puckish face of my professor, his short hair parted neatly

in the middle and combed down over his forehead, his eyes blinking incessantly behind steel-rimmed spectacles as though he had just emerged into strong light, his lips nibbling each other like nervous horses, his smile shuttling to and fro in a carefully edged mustache.

This is a short description and yet, from his "puckish face" to his "hair parted neatly" and "carefully edged mustache," we have an unforgettable portrait of a man who was devoted to preserving the purity of the English language.

William Faulkner opens his story "Old Man" (from *Three Famous Short Novels*, Random House) with this description: "Once . . . there were two convicts. One of them was about twenty-five, tall, lean and flat-stomached, with a sunburned face and Indian-black hair and pale, china-colored outraged eyes." It is the outrage expressed in his eyes to which Faulkner devotes his story.

Or, turn to Hemingway's great short story, "The Killers" (from *Men Without Women*, Scribner's). His first sentence sets the stage: "The door of Henry's lunch-room opened and two men came in. They sat down at the counter." A brief dialogue follows as the two gangsters wrangle with the counterman over what they will eat; then the description:

"I'll take ham and eggs," the man called Al said. He wore a derby and a black overcoat buttoned across the chest. His face was small and white and he had tight lips. He wore a silk muffler and gloves.

"Give me bacon and eggs," said the other man. He was about the same size as Al. Their faces were different, but they were dressed like twins. Both wore overcoats too tight for them. They sat, leaning forward, their elbows on the counter.

Sometimes a single physical characteristic gives an unforgettable picture, as when Virginia Woolf in *A Writer's Diary* (Harcourt, Brace & Co.) says, "I noticed how his hair is every blade of it white, with some space between the blades: a very sparsely sown field."

Physical peculiarities often make an indelible impression. Truman Capote in *In Cold Blood* (Random House) refers again and again to Perry Smith's short legs and to Dick Hitchcock's off-balance face. And who can forget Uriah Heep's clammy hands? Dickens first tells us that he had "a long, lank, skeleton hand." Later, "what a clammy hand his was! Ghostly to the touch as to the sight! I rubbed mine afterwards to warm it, and *to rub his off*."

Hands and their mannerisms are often dead giveaways to a person. One of my students used them to good purpose as an exercise of description. He is speaking of a Chinese citizen he had met abroad:

He looked away in embarrassment as his limp hand folded in my grasp—I had not known then that the Chinese regard handshaking as too personal and so somewhat vulgar. . . . He lowered himself slowly into the chair, placed his elbows on the armrests and folded his soft, manicured fingers across his chest.

What kind of person is he?

A quick index of character—to be expanded later in the article—often comes on the heels of the physical description. I followed this pattern in a profile of Queen Frederika of Greece which I wrote for *McCall's* some years ago. The article opened:

> Like her distant cousin, Elizabeth of England, Queen Frederika of Greece is small, young and extraordinarily pretty. But there the resemblance ends. Elizabeth is cool and aloof, a queen in the story book tradition. Frederika, with her curls, her dimples, her crinkled grin, is warm, fun-loving, dynamic, an energetic citizen of the here and now.

Her personality is hinted there; it is elaborated in the second paragraph:

> If she had gone to an American college, Frederika could have been voted most popular girl on campus. She probably would have run for student government, and occasionally been called down to the dean's office. "I can't resist sticking my nose into everything," she admits. If she had not found herself Queen of Greece, she might have been an adored nursery school teacher, or the able administrative head of a woman's college. For she has a deep love and understanding of children and young people, a passionate interest in getting things done for them and a capacity for getting what she wants.

The purpose of this profile was to show the queen's relation to her children and to picture her as a mother. So the characteristics stressed are the ones that reflect that side of her personality. If the article had concerned itself with her role in the politics of her country, different traits would have been emphasized.

What does he say, and how does he talk?

As is evident in the last chapter, how people talk and what they say reveal their personality traits and characteristics. Use direct quotes wherever possible. For example, "Governor Long's nephew said that his uncle was wearing his years well," is a dull statement as contrasted with " 'Uncle Earl's still got a lot of snap left in his garters,' said his nephew." The quote gives a colorful picture not only of the Governor, but of the Long clan.

Compare, "He said he didn't like modern apartment buildings," with, "Anybody who says he'd like to live in one of those damned little boxes with cardboard walls is a humbug—or a renting agent." This, too, tells much about the talker. So don't go into a Nice Nelly act and take all the zip out of the conversation. A speaker's hesitations and repetitions, his unfinished sentences, even his invectives are part of his makeup. Listen for them and use them.

How he acts

The actions and reactions of your subject make up the main body of your profile, usually taking up ninety per cent of the space. It is in this way that you build up, step by step, the picture of your hero's life that you wish to portray. Your success will depend on the incidents you select. The simple rule is that you must include only incidents that will further the theme of your article.

As an example, here is an outline of a profile of Miss Fanny, who taught a small private school in a southern town in the early years of this century. The school was one

room in a house she occupied with her mother and sister
who took in sewing, and the pupils ranged in age from five-
and-a-half to twelve. The purpose of the article is to show
that before educators had set up a pattern for producing
secure and well-adjusted children, Miss Fanny was intuitively practicing what is now considered good pedagogy;
although she had never finished high school, she communicated her own thirst for learning to her pupils. These are
the incidents selected:

1. Miss Fanny went to call on the parents of a new pupil
before school opened to meet and reassure the child. This
was not usual then.

2. On the first day of school, she gave each new pupil a
place of his own—a small chair to fit the child and a new
slate and pencil and pictures cut from magazines—to make
the child feel at home.

3. At recess, if a child did not know the games the older
children were playing, she took him aside and taught him
to skip rope, for instance. So the child became "adjusted
to his peer group," as we say now.

4. Miss Fanny had her sister teach the first graders how
to count from strings of brightly colored buttons, so arithmetic became an absorbing game.

5. Miss Fanny never shamed a child by exposing his
faults in public. When a country boy was the butt of the
town children because of his ungrammatical expressions,
she set her other pupils at some task, while she had quiet
little conversations with him and explained about the use
of "isn't" instead of "ain't," and "you" instead of "you'uns."
Afterwards she had him tell stories of life on the farm so
that his schoolmates accepted him with new respect for his
abilities.

6. Occasionally Miss Fanny invited the parents to her house for lemonade and cookies in the evening, so they could talk about their children. That was before the days of the PTA.

7. Miss Fanny taught her pupils to love books. On a spring day, she would say, "If you get your arithmetic and spelling done this morning, we can spend the afternoon reading." Then she took her pupils out under the cherry tree and read *Little Women* and *Little Men* and *David Copperfield* aloud. So they worked like beavers in the mornings at the three R's and could hardly wait for the next reading session. To those who had no books at home, she lent her own or borrowed for them from a Sunday School library. She opened a new world for her children.

8. When, in her own reading, Miss Fanny discovered a new subject, she shared it with her pupils. She found a book on astronomy and asked the parents to bring their children to her back yard on a starry night and pointed out the stars and planets. The next day she read to the school about them.

9. After her pupils had gone on to public school, she invited those who were not doing well to her house on a Saturday afternoon, and made the geography or history or grammar so simple and interesting they went back to their dull classes with confidence. There were no dropouts among Miss Fanny's graduates.

There were many other incidents available about Miss Fanny's life, but they had no place in this short article and were not included. The piece moves on to the end when, many years afterwards, a pupil who had made a name for himself as an educator, wrote her, "My children have the advantages of the new teaching methods in the best school in our city, but I wish they were getting the love of learning you gave me in your little school."

With no college, no normal school, no teachers' college behind her, Miss Fanny emerges as a great and lovable teacher.

What do other people think of him?

The opinions of your central character's family, associates, friends or enemies will round out your picture of him. Although these may be introduced at many points in your article, they are often used with excellent effect as a final summing up. This was done effectively by Jean Libman Block in a profile of her uncle, Dr. Emanuel Libman, in the *Reader's Digest* (December, 1964):

> On his sixtieth birthday his former students—his children in medicine—decided to honor him by publishing a testimonial volume of medical papers. The response from friends and disciples was so tremendous that the one volume grew to three, containing 130 papers contributed by outstanding scientists from 18 countries . . . Perhaps the greatest tribute paid Uncle Manny came from his friend Alexis Carrel. "Libman," he said, "is medicine itself."

If your subject is a controversial public figure, opinions for and against him are a dime a dozen. You find them in newspapers, magazines, even from the man in the street. Occasionally when you are writing of a person not well known, but important in his own circle, you may find that no one wants to say a critical word.

That was my experience when I was writing a piece on a woman who, before her death, had built up an important business. From all the people I talked with she emerged a saintly figure—a good wife, a loving mother, a doting grandmother, a kind and generous employer. I had met her once and remembered her as a salty, even peppery, old lady. But I could find no support for this. Finally I tracked down one of her contemporaries, a woman, now retired, who had worked with her from her early and struggling days. A long telephone conversation gave me a new picture:

"She certainly had a will of her own," my source said. "Days when she marched into her office without so much as a good day to anyone, we all knew was no time to cross her. I'll tell you those days everybody walked on eggs. We'd find out afterwards that someone had been trying to put a shady deal over on her. When she'd won out, sugar wouldn't melt in her mouth."

This was what I needed to show that her success had come because she had been a good fighter.

Unrevealed traits of a person can sometimes be told by indirection. One of my students accomplished this very neatly in an exercise to portray a person in a hundred words:

The first time I saw Mrs. Scott, my sister and I were having dinner in her restaurant, *The Arm and Hammer*. She came into the dining room, all hundred and eighty pounds of her, pink face, gray hair around her head in braids, large coral earrings that looked somehow like tropical fish clinging to her ear lobes. She was wearing a simple white linen dress, white pumps and went from table to table, saying, "Enjoyin' youah dinnah?" My sister looked in her direction. "That must be Mrs. Arm," she offered. Then, "Or Mrs. Hammer, maybe."

Often a single pungent line is worth a page of description, as, for example, Eugenia Sheppard's item in the *New York Herald Tribune* (November 14, 1965): "New York ladies at charity balls often behave as if they were frozen and preserved inside their diamonds." And again, Joyce Porter in her detective novel, *Dover 2*: "He didn't believe in keeping a dog and barking himself."

In another item, a New Yorker in a rage over the fine old buildings being torn down to make room for new steel and glass skyscrapers says: "Park Avenue looks like a slit in a glacier."

Or Mary Margaret McBride's comment in a profile of her friend and business manager: "Stella Karn blew into my life like a whirlwind." (*Reader's Digest,* January, 1962).

Word portraits

You will find many more examples of all kinds of description in your own reading, and I recommend that you set yourself to look for these word portraits, and learn from them how to use what you observe. But don't paraphrase and pass on as your own someone else's description, however apt it may be. You would be using second-hand material and any discerning editor would spot it. Besides it will lack the freshness of your own newly-minted impressions.

Some writers are born with talents for keen observation and with photographic memories. They are lucky. But those of us who are not so blessed need not despair. You

can teach yourself to observe just as you can teach yourself to become a good listener. Give yourself little exercises: when you walk into a room look around, then close
your eyes and see if you can describe it to yourself and
enumerate what is in it. If not, try again. When you meet
a person, size him up. What characteristic makes him different or unique? What is your first impression? Then
mentally go into details on his height, clothes, mannerisms. Take time, when you are at leisure, to find precise
descriptive words for his looks. When you are eating alone
at a restaurant is an excellent time to do this, or when you
are riding on a bus, train or plane. Keep it up and you
will find yourself making these mental notes automatically.
As your sensibilities are alerted you will have the bonus
of finding more pleasure in life.

I once went driving in the spring with a great reporter.
Even though he was at the wheel, his eye caught every
sign of spring along the road. When we returned, he could
make the trip memorable for those who stayed at home.

For yourself, remember that if you don't see, you can't
convey the sight to your reader, and what the reader can't
see, he may not believe. If your memory is faulty, make
up for it by taking notes. Practice will sharpen your ability to remember.

Do you like him?

At some point when you are interviewing your subject
and others who know him and when you are collecting
facts about him, you will find yourself making your own
appraisal of him. Do you like him? Do you find him admirable in some way? Objectionable in others? Why?

To find the answers, you may need to look into his

background and upbringing and the forces or circumstances which may have influenced him. In other words, you need to know him well. You may find that you have approached him with a preconceived idea and that it has changed as you came to know more and more about him.

In any case, by the time you are ready to begin writing, you should have formed your own opinion and be ready to ask yourself, "What impression of him do I want to leave with the reader?" On the answer will depend the mood of your piece, the selections you will make from your notes, incidents, quotes, even physical description. Say, "she is well-rounded," and you convey a pleasant impression; say, "she's fat," a critical one. Compare "carefully groomed" with "finicky about his looks."

To prove to yourself your ability to awake an emotional response from your reader, practice the following: In about a hundred words describe a person you know well, using quotes, action and description to achieve these different effects:

1. Show him (or her) as a pleasant person
2. As an unpleasant person
3. As pleasant on the whole but with some human failings.

The third is the one you will probably use most often—few people are all good or all bad and even a person whom you are holding up as admirable becomes more believable if you include some lapses from grace.

To return to your profile: remember that a mere collection of incidents, related one after the other will not make a well-rounded, believable portrait. Each bit of description, characterization, incident, anecdote or action must be related to the other and must contribute to the purpose of your article; otherwise, you will have a hodge-podge that leads nowhere. A short example: In the article on Mrs. Roosevelt's home life, mentioned earlier, the writer noted that Mrs. Roosevelt's favorite dessert was Jell-o. This took its place in the portrait because Jell-o is a simple dessert, often associated with children, so it became a small but expressive detail that added to the theme of simplicity the writer aimed for. If the favorite dessert had been chocolate mousse, which the President's wife would have met often in dining out, it would have meant nothing to this article and would not have been included.

To repeat: when you are planning your article, do have a clear picture of the impression you want to leave with the reader. Then, with your notes before you, discard anything that is not relevant. Don't get on your horse and ride off in all directions. Know your objective and ride the straight road toward it.

A place you know

You will find that your writing will take on more authority and you will be more at home with your characters if you base your descriptions on people and places you know well. But do look at your neighbors with a fresh eye and listen to them with an attentive ear. How do they talk? How do they live? What is individual about them? Even in regimented United States where to the casual eye every Main Street is like every other Main Street, where every teen-ager follows the same fads, where the slum in New York has its counterpart in Los Angeles and the country club set in Ohio is hardly distinguishable from

that in Detroit or Connecticut—even amid all this seem-
ing sameness, individuality is to be found, each person
has something that is unique to himself. Look for it.

You have plenty of precedent for making your own environment the scene of your articles. In fiction, Faulkner,
a southerner, writes about the south; Mary Ellen Chase, a
down-easterner, writes of New England; the young New
Yorkers picture the people about them. Somerset Maugham
in the second sentence of his *The Summing Up* says,
"In one way or another I have used in my writings whatever has happened to me in the course of my life." Successful non-fiction writers also start from a home base.

So map out your own territory. Your picture of it will
be more original and have more meaning than a tale of
some place you've never been or of a person, however
notable, whom you've never seen.

ℵ 10

POINT OF VIEW

STILL ANOTHER DECISION will face you before you face your typewriter to begin an article—or for that matter a short story or novel: from whose point of view will you write your piece? Through whose eyes is the person or action seen? Who is the narrator? You have several choices.

It happened to me

You can write in the first person—the "I" story. The personal experience or the "it happened to me" article immediately comes to mind. And its twin, the profile of the "Unforgettable Character" type in which the author is directly involved with the person he is writing about. Turn the pages of a number of magazines and you will find that "I" and "we" are the narrators of pieces on many subjects. For instance, travel and adventure articles in which the author tells of some interesting or amusing or perilous experience he had; articles of advice on everything from finance to burping the baby; articles of opinion, usually from an authority; how-to-do-it pieces, reminiscences, commentaries, criticism.

In any of these, you are describing a person, an event or series of events, a situation, an emotion or a belief in which you are personally involved. You describe what you did or what was done to you, what you saw or what you believe and its effect on you or on someone you know or have observed.

If you use the first person, you should have experienced or witnessed the main events and should have had easy-to-come-by knowledge of others. Do not include anything of which you do not have personal knowledge.

Third person

You can write in the third person from a single point of view. Take a subject that is much in the news—the high school dropout. Depending on the purpose of your article, you could write it from any one of many points of view. You could write from the standpoint of a boy who has dropped out and tell of the pressures that affected him and boys like him. Or through the eyes of a parent—perhaps a father who had set his heart on his boy's going to college. Where had he slipped up? Or as the school principal sees the problem; he watches a score of such boys every year. What does he think? Or from the angle of the social worker or juvenile court judge who takes over when these boys get into trouble. You might even want to write from the point of view of a domestic Peace Corps worker, who thinks that all is not lost. He has known boys who have gone back to night school, finished up and become successful and happy.

In each case you would have a different purpose. From

the boy's point of view, you might want to show that the family or home background was at fault; from the parent's, that our system of child rearing needs an overhauling; from the principal's, that we need better schools and more teachers.

As in the first-person piece, preserve the unity of your article by sticking to what your narrator sees and thinks and feels.

You can write in the third person from more than one point of view. As an example, there is the popular "Can this marriage be saved?" article about the couple whose marriage is breaking up. They seek the help of a marriage counselor, who is the narrator. After an introduction, the counselor tells of the conflict from the wife's point of view, often quoting her own words. Then he tells of his interviews with the husband and gives these to us in a similar fashion. In conclusion, the counselor sums up the pros and cons, tells what his advice was and finally whether or not the marriage was saved.

Or suppose you are writing about a mountain climbing adventure. You open the article when the climbers are leaving the lodge, and you follow them through the day, telling the story through the eyes of a young man who is a member of the party. In the middle of the afternoon, something goes wrong—a slide or an accident. The climbers are stranded and need help.

Shifts and transitions

Then with a transition sentence that says in effect, "Meanwhile at the lodge," you shift back and show what is happening through the eyes of someone there, perhaps the wife of another climber. She has been anxiously awaiting their return. At her plea, a rescue party is organized, and she sets out with them. Then, using another transition sentence—"Up on the mountain. . . ."—you return to the climbers and finish the piece from the viewpoint of the original young man.

This can be very effective in building and holding suspense, and if the reader identifies himself with the narrator, can result in a moving or exciting article. Make sure that the reader knows when you have shifted and is always conscious of who is speaking.

Make as few shifts as possible. If you go shuttling back and forth, you lose impetus and confuse the reader. Think of each point of view as an episode that comes to a climax before you shift to another. In the mountain climbing piece, the first episode covers the start of the climb up to and through the accident, and the climbers' desperate need for help. The second takes place at the lodge, shows the concern of those waiting, the rescue party and their success in finding the climbers. The third episode tells of the return of the party and their relief at the rescue or their disappointment at not succeeding in the climb (whichever it is).

In a manuscript of book length, it is possible to make a number of shifts; often each one indicated by a new chapter. An excellent example of skillful handling of such an adventure is *PT 109, John F. Kennedy in World War II* by Robert J. Donovan.

The main section of the book is devoted to the destruction of PT 109 by a Japanese destroyer and the heroic efforts of its skipper, young John Kennedy, to save his crew. Each night a small fleet of PT's, including 109, patrolled a passage among the Pacific islands along which Japanese ships ran to provision and arm an island air strip. The adventure starts when the PT 109 and its fellows leave their base for the night patrol and recounts the incidents and hazards along the way. It shifts quickly to three Japanese destroyers on their mission, then returns to Kennedy and his crew and their separation from the other PT's; back again to the Japanese destroyer which has sighted the small boat and run it down, cutting it in two, but leaving the foredeck afloat.

Then again to PT 109, surrounded by flaming oil on the water: the men overboard, Kennedy's rescue of a badly burned seaman; their climb back onto the sinking boat; the crew's take-off from the sinking boat, Kennedy with the burned seaman on his back; the long swim to a nearby island; the wait for rescue; the move to another island; the swims out into the channel at night in hopes of interception by a PT patrol—no luck.

Now a shift to an Australian coast watcher on an island peak; his discovery of the shipwrecked men, his radio message to the base. Back to Kennedy and his crew; the coming of friendly natives in a canoe who take off for the base with a message Kennedy has scratched on a coconut shell. And finally the rescue.

Each episode came to a climax before another was begun. The point of view centered on Kennedy with quick shifts to the destroyer, the coast watcher, and the base command as the action demanded. The author prepared the reader for each shift and the reader was never in doubt as to where he was.

An excellent example of a novel told from various points of view is *The Rector of Justin* by Louis Auchincloss. The Rector is the revered head of a boys' boarding school.

The book opens with an account of the Rector by a young teacher, who finds him wholly exemplary. There follows, chapter by chapter, reminiscences of the Rector by many others who had known him during his life: the chairman of the school's board of trustees, a former schoolmate, a boy the Rector had flunked, an admirer of his wife, his daughter and others. At the end you have a rounded portrait of the man, his faults and his follies, his strengths and his virtues.

You can write your article entirely from the omniscient point of view. Here the author can be everywhere at once; he knows everything pertinent about everyone he introduces; he is able to get inside the minds of any character and to know what he is doing and thinking. Using the omniscient point of view successfully requires great skill, especially when you are writing articles about people, and I would not advise a beginning writer to use this technique in writing a profile.

However, in these post-Freudian days when many writers consider themselves psychiatrists, it is possible. But if the reader is to have any identification with the character or feel that he is present at the scene, the author might better show his character in action and not go into a long exploration of his psyche. Better leave that for fiction.

This omniscient viewpoint is, however, good for an article on something inanimate, such as a city, some new invention, or even political and historical articles where the writer has collected material from many different sources and wishes to cover all sides of a question.

א 11

PATTERN AND STRUCTURE—
BUILDING THE ARTICLE

THERE COMES A TIME when the preliminary work is done. You have collected your facts from reading and from interviewing; you have a store of pertinent anecdotes and authentic quotes; and you have a sheaf of notes. You are convinced that your facts will make an article, and that your subject will answer the reader's question of "What's in it for me?" You have decided on the type of magazine that would be interested in your story.

If your story is a profile, a clear picture of your subject and your own opinion of him have taken shape in your mind. Whatever your article, you know from what point of view you will tell your story and the thought you wish to leave with your reader.

The time has come to arrange the miscellaneous material you have gathered into an orderly whole. "Any piece of handwork," says William A. H. Birnie, senior editor of the *Reader's Digest,* "if it is to have any excellence must have a certain form and a progression. Otherwise it is chaotic." A mere collection of facts, incidents, anecdotes and quotes, however interesting, does not make an article. They must be arranged in such a way that the article moves in a straight line from the beginning, through the middle, to the end. This arrangement is called the structure, and it supports your piece as the framing supports a house. Without it, your piece is like a jerry-built hovel which will collapse with the first strong wind.

Four-part pattern

Today's articles usually follow a simple four-part pattern:

1. *The lead* which catches the reader's eye and lures him into the subject. It should give a hint of what is to follow.

2. *The theme* of the article, sometimes called the *slant,* is the paragraph that immediately follows the lead. This tells what you want to say about the subject—your point of view. Either in the lead or the theme paragraph you should indicate the reader's stake in the piece.

3. *The body* or main portion of your article. Here you build up your theme with facts, examples and anecdotes, so that as your article moves along it informs the reader and leaves him with the knowledge or impression you want to put across.

4. *The conclusion,* which may be a summary, or a final anecdote that ties up your theme, or it may be a restatement of your theme. Your ending should be a strong one —you don't want your piece to peter out—and it should leave the reader with a feeling of satisfaction. S. S. McClure neatly defined the good article when he said that it

"is a collection of facts so arranged that the reader inevitably arrives at a conclusion which fortunately he thinks his own."

The following article, *Reading Writing*, by Theodore Irwin from *Coronet* (March, 1966) illustrates the structural pattern:

READING WRITING

by Theodore Irwin

It could have happened to you, and it did to a well-educated housewife in Montclair, N.J. The night before, she had scribbled a note to her milkman, asking him to leave three quarts of chocolate milk. Next morning on her doorstep she found eight cartons of cottage cheese. The milkman had made a poor guess at her handwriting.

In Philadelphia, the Central Penn National Bank carries a special "Who Am I?" account to which is credited money from deposit slips on which the name of the depositor cannot be deciphered. At times the "Who Am I?" balance has mounted to as much as $50,000.

Awareness that we've become a nation of scrawlers is evidenced by admonitions to "print" our names and addresses on government forms such as driving licenses and income tax returns. It has even penetrated the realm of soul-saving. At meetings where evangelist Billy Graham calls for converts and ushers to pass out cards to the audience, he invariably pleads: "Please, my friends, please *print* on your cards. It will save us hours of work."

Our handwriting seems to be getting worse each year, especially as we rely more and more on the telephone, typewriter, dictating machine, electronic robots and secretaries. For most of us, calligraphy or penmanship has become as obsolete as smoke signals.

Our dismal failure to mind our p's and q's pops up everywhere we turn. The Internal Revenue Service, for instance, finds it impossible to process about half a million refund checks a year because the taxpayers' writing of amounts, names or addresses is hopelessly illegible. The Veterans Administration has had to produce a special film showing the delays and losses to veterans because V.A. employees don't write so that they can be read. Every year the Post Office consigns about 25 million "nixies" to dead letter offices because of poorly written addresses.

If you can't read your wife's shopping list (is that "cufflinks" or "cornflakes"?) or the inscrutable hieroglyphics on a waiter's check, consider the havoc in business and industry. One survey estimated that undecipherable records, orders and instructions are costing the United States economy at least a million and a half dollars a week. Automation, instead of preventing snafus, actually compounds the trouble. At one big oil company, a card-punch operator who misread a poorly written number made 3,000 wrong invoices.

You've probably had your own unfortunate experiences with department stores, perhaps receiving a girdle instead of a griddle. To combat hard-to-read names and addresses on sales checks, the charge-a-plate was introduced years ago. Still, stores like J. L. Hudson's in Detroit found that more than 20,000 sales slips were being held up each year because of poor writing. One customer who ordered "sleepers with grippers" for her baby received a pair of "slippers with zippers."

Deliveries are often made difficult by handwritingitis. According to United Parcel Service, every day, in one city alone, about 1,200 packages are undeliverable because drivers can't make head or tail of the addresses. To educate the stores' employees, United Parcel has sent out posters, one showing a museum curator deciding that the hieroglyphics on a package are Sanskrit. All, apparently, in vain. The other day, a black chiffon nightgown, size 12, was delivered to a 64-year-old, 200 pound lady in Stamford, Conn., who had ordered a hot-water bottle!

Other delivery men have similar woes. In Washington, D.C., not long ago, a truck driver wasn't sure if it was a "1" or a "7" on a handwritten order and proceeded to pump 260 gallons of fuel oil through a disconnected intake—flooding the basement of the wrong house.

You'd think that telephone companies wouldn't care about poor handwriting but they, too, suffer from it. Particularly on long-distance calls, thousands of dollars are lost every month when illegible toll tickets have to be tossed out rather than chance an inaccurate charge. A scribbled exchange abbreviation can be read as either CA (for CAnal) or CO (for COlumbus), and a customer billed for a long-distance call to Albuquerque hits the ceiling because no one in his family knows anyone in Albuquerque.

Banks, too, are highly vulnerable to unreadable writing. With bookkeepers developing neuroses trying to identify signatures, most banks have introduced checks with the customer's name imprinted on them. Still, handwriting gives some tellers the jitters.

Not long ago in Boston, a man stepped up to a teller's window and shoved a note under the wicket. On it was scrawled something that looked like "Mzg I hdkz a mww czvqpt8mr!" Scared stiff, the teller kicked his alarm button, bells went off, guards dashed up and collared the "hold-up man." The poor fellow turned out to be an honest merchant with a sore throat. He had meant his note to read, "May I have a new checkbook?"

It's a toss-up who has the worst penmanship. One survey of secretaries found that the handwriting of fully half of our executives is either "hard to read" or "downright impossible." Low on the totem pole are aviation executives, insurance men and chemical engineers. One secretary in an advertising agency complained that her boss wrote "like an Egyptian in the reign of Rameses II."

By far the most notorious is the extraordinary calligraphy of doctors. In the words of a professor at the Columbia College of Pharmacy:

"The average druggist must stand on his head at least once a day, trying to read what a doctor has written. Then, apologetically, he phones the doctor, perhaps using a subterfuge, saying that the patient spilled water on the prescription and made it illegible."

The classic yarn about medical handwriting, probably apocryphal, concerns the spider that fell into a doctor's inkwell, crawled out and walked aimlessly over a prescription pad, leaving intricate track marks. A nurse, mistaking the sheet for a prescription, sent it to a druggist. After studying the "prescription" for a while, the druggist called up the doctor. "Doc," he said, "I'm sorry, but this new prescription stumps me. I can't figure out the last word you wrote."

The following incident did actually occur in Yonkers, N.Y. A stranger walked into a drugstore and handed the pharmacist, William Astmann, a prescription for a narcotic. Astmann glanced at it, felt something was wrong, and told the man the prescription would be ready in an hour. Then he phoned the doctor. It turned out that the customer, an addict, had stolen a prescription pad from the doctor's office and forged a blank. What had sparked the pharmacist's suspicion? "That prescription," the druggist said, "was too clear to have been written by any legitimate doctor."

In the drug industry, so many errors were made on orders taken by salesmen (is it "Benzedrine" or "Benadryl"?) that an expert was assigned to work up a 152-page text for drug salesmen to help insure accuracy.

One never knows when or where, in our private lives, bad handwriting can prove costly. It may mean the difference between landing a job or being passed over. Notice, for instance, that many help-wanted ads ask the applicant to "reply in own handwriting." Most corporations regard good handwriting as a vital factor in appraising job seekers. As one personnel manager put it, "People who fill out applications in a sloppy way are apt to be inaccurate and lazy on the job."

Obviously, the most common causes of poor handwriting are haste and carelessness—and then the sloppy writing becomes a habit. The chief faults are failure to close *o*'s, dot *i*'s and cross *t*'s. Most poor writers also improperly form the letters *e*, *n*, *d*, *r*, *a*, *h* and *b*, especially in making loops on letters that shouldn't have loops, such as *t* and *i*. Most frequently confused are the letters *o* and *a*, and *u* and *v*. Auditors find that most mistakes in numerals occur with *1* and *7*, as well as with *3*, *5* and *8*.

Behind the loss of the art of handwriting is not so much the rise in typing; after all, we have to sign our name and address or write a note often during the day. More basic is the lack in our educational system. Starting in the depression years, economy-minded schools cut penmanship teachers from the payroll and later never put them back. Teachers' colleges, stressing general education rather than classroom techniques, turned out few graduates qualified to teach handwriting. Result: the second "R" is no longer being adequately taught.

Even school teachers today often have atrocious handwriting. One authority, Prof. C. W. Hunnicutt of Syracuse University, conducted a survey a few years ago which elicited this comment from an outstanding educator:

"One of the biggest drawbacks to teaching pupils to write well is the very poor handwriting of the majority of new teachers who come into our school system. Most have had no handwriting courses in their teacher training. Their board writing is scarcely legible, and their desire to improve is negligible."

Handwriting supervisors and teachers have virtually disappeared. In the 1920's there were over 500. Today, in the entire state of Texas, only one town has a special handwriting supervisor. Wisconsin has one and California has none at all.

Dr. Luella Cole, former professor of educational psychology at the University of Indiana, issued this indictment:

"Everywhere I have gone, I have found handwriting the worst-taught, the most neglected and the least-understood subject in the elementary school."

Many children are asked to do too much writing before they've mastered the manual dexterity. Writing requires fine muscular control—the coordination of about 500 different muscles is involved—and children get tired and tense. School schedules are too crowded nowadays with other subjects, so that less attention is paid to handwriting in the curriculum and less time spent on practice. Moreover, there's lack of motivation among youngsters. One high school junior said he didn't give a darn about his handwriting: "I intend to have a secretary."

However, lately a resurgence of interest in improved handwriting has been noticed. Some schools now have in-service workshops for new teachers where they are helped to write legibly both on the board and on paper. The New England School Development Council has appointed a handwriting committee which developed a teachers' guide, "Handwriting Today," to revitalize penmanship programs.

In Philadelphia, after businessmen complained about the deplorable handwriting of the city's high school graduates, officials came up with a "Philadelphia Simplified Alphabet"— a new method by which youngsters are now learning to write. Misleading "scrollwork" is eliminated; t's contain no loop; care is taken to distinguish between look-alike numerals.

Television programs on educational networks have been used in Cleveland, Des Moines and Alabama, directed not only to teachers and upper-grade students but also to "downtown business girls." In Tucson, Ariz., awards are now being given to elementary school pupils for superior handwriting and there's even a "Good Writers Club." Pittsburgh has an "Improve Your Handwriting Month."

Business and industry, too, are taking action. In their running battle against poor handwritingitis, department stores send a credit man around to a guilty department with a fistful of incomprehensible sales checks. As the slips are passed around among the clerks, the credit man asks, "What do you think they mean?" Handwriting is now part of the sales training in many stores. At some stores in New York, salesclerks are being taught to print "because apparently they never learned to write." Packages with labels not block-printed are stopped at the wrapping department. At special staff meetings, prizes are offered for the first person to decipher a particularly maddening sales check.

To cut down their losses, telephone companies have brought in penmanship experts to hold classes for toll and long-lines operators. To reduce medication errors, handwriting courses are being given to our leading culprits—the doctors.

Would you like to improve your own handwriting? Here are some simple rules:

Analyze your own handwriting for its faults. Use more care in forming letters and numerals. Avoid crowding. Always remember that, unless you're confiding in your diary, you expect someone else to read your prose.

"With care," Prof. Hunnicutt assures us, "any person who truly wants to, can write legibly."

If you do take the trouble to improve your handwriting, better notify your bank and all your credit-card organizations. One New York lawyer who started sedulously watching his p's and q's received a call from his bank one morning.

"I have a check with your name signed to it," said the teller, "and it doesn't match your signature card. I believe it's a forgery."

The lawyer rushed to the bank. It turned out that the signature on the check was indeed his own. What confused the teller was that now it was actually legible!

Analysis

The lead makes an immediate bid for the reader's attention by its opening sentence: "It could have happened to you, and it did to a well-educated housewife in Montclair, N.J." The author follows the housewife's experience with a second example—the bank—which has wider implications.

The theme is stated in the third paragraph which begins, "Awareness that we've become a nation of scrawlers is evidenced by admonitions to 'print' our names and addresses on government forms, such as driving licenses and income tax returns," and extends even to the realm of soul-saving as illustrated by Billy Graham's plea.

The body of the article is introduced with "Our handwriting seems to be getting worse each year." It takes up in order A) the results of poor handwriting and its cost to the economy; B) the culprits, the causes, hope for the future; C) how you can improve your own handwriting. Here is a detailed outline of the body of the article:

A. Results of poor handwriting and cost:
  1. Internal revenue unable to make refunds to taxpayers and veterans
  2. Post office unable to deliver letters
  3. Undecipherable records, orders, etc.
     Cost to economy estimated at million and a half dollars a week

B. Some of the culprits
   1. Department store sales people who make out unde-
      cipherable sales' slips and delivery addresses. Trou-
      bles of United Parcel Service and other delivery
      men
   2. Telephone company employees
   3. Depositors at banks
   4. Executives
   5. Doctors—illegible prescriptions
   6. Drug company salesmen whose poor handwriting
      results in deliveries of wrong drugs

C. Cost to us in our private lives
   This is a transitional paragraph which brings home to
   each of us the personal cost of poor handwriting, and
   leads into the next topic with its last sentence: "As one
   personnel manager put it, 'People who fill out applications in a sloppy way are apt to be inaccurate and lazy
   on the job.' "

D. Causes of poor handwriting
   1. Haste and carelessness. This is introduced by: "Ob-
      viously, the most common causes of poor handwrit-
      ing are haste and carelessness—and then the sloppy
      writing becomes a habit." Notice how the repeti-
      tion of the word "sloppy" ties this in with the
      preceding paragraph.
   2. The defects in our educational system
      a. Economy which dismisses handwriting teach-
         ers
      b. Teachers colleges which do not train hand-
         writing teachers
      c. Teachers with poor handwriting
      d. Children are asked to do too much hand-

writing before they have mastered manual dexterity

E. Hope for the future. Transitional sentence: "However, lately a resurgence of interest in improved handwriting has been noticed." Examples:
 1. Some grade schools
 2. Philadelphia high schools
 3. Educational TV programs
 4. Business—handwriting stressed in training programs

F. How to improve your handwriting. Transitional sentence: "Would you like to improve your own handwriting? Here are some simple rules . . ."

The conclusion opens with, "If you do take the trouble to improve your handwriting," introduces a new thought and ends with an amusing anecdote.

That is a neat and obvious pattern. One section moves easily to the next and the whole gives such an effortless effect that you might think anyone could do it.

And yet many a writer, whether he is experienced or a beginner, when finally confronted with his sheaf of notes, often feels that he will never be able to bring order into them. If you are one of these writers, there are various ways to get over that hurdle.

How to proceed

You may want to use chronological order, which is often effective whether you are writing about a person or tracing the development of a particular topic. Take again our aspiring Senator about whose college days you are writing. You might sort your notes in the following order:

1. His background (parents and ancestors)
2. His boyhood
3. His high school years
4. The reasons for his choice of college
5. His first year, second, third and fourth. Since this is the main part of your article, you might prefer to sub-divide this section under his sports, his academic work, his social life, or whatever
6. His graduation
7. His first steps thereafter
8. And finally the effect of his college education on his career

If your notes are typed, you will sort the sheets under each of your headings. If a sheet covers more than one heading, cut it apart so you can put each note under its proper head. Transfer each group of notes to a separate folder. Then each folder will contain all the facts, anecdotes, quotes and odd bits and pieces that are pertinent to that period of his life.

If your notes are still in your notebook and you have taken them down as you have done the research and interviewing, so that sometimes there are two or three subjects to the page, try this system: Make a list of the headings on a separate sheet of paper. Go through the notebooks with your list before you. When you find a paragraph that should be included under number 1, put the figure 1 in the margin of the page. Then proceed with 2, 3, 4, and so on.

When you begin to write, as you come to each topic,

look for its number in your notebook and cover it in your first draft. This method makes it easy to find the notes pertinent to each period or topic and insures that you will not forget or misquote an item.

This first sequence of folders or numbers does not mean that you will necessarily follow their order in your article. For your "college days" piece, you might begin at any point in his career. If you decided to start with his first day at college, your first sentence might read: "The raw-boned country boy in the new bright blue suit, his knobby hands dangling from too-short sleeves, was first in line at the registration desk of University of Kentucky on September 19th, 1942." After identifying him, you might flash back to his background (#1) or his boyhood (#2) which leads to his college days, and go forward from that.

Or you might want to introduce him as he is today or begin with his graduation from college or wherever you have an attention-getting incident. You might even go back to his ancestors with a start like this: "If Big Joe Arnold, when he limped back to Breathitt County, Kentucky, after Appomattox, had thought that one day his great-grandson would go down to the Bluegrass for book larnin', he would. . . ."

If your piece does not lend itself to a chronological sequence, then sort your notes under whatever headings they seem to fit logically. If you had been writing "Reading Writing," you might have used headings like this:

1. Our handwriting today is abominable. Examples
2. Why?   Haste and carelessness
           Our educational system
3. What is being done about it?

4. What are the results of it? Examples
5. What is it costing the country?
6. What is it costing us?
7. How can we make it better?

This is not, as you have observed, the order which the writer followed. You will often find that the order you finally arrive at emerges during the actual writing. The purpose of this first sorting is simply to make sure of the topics you will cover and that you have the material that applies to each topic all together where you can find it easily without leafing through all your notes. Your list of topics also serves as a sort of free-wheeling outline.

At this point, some writers can see the direction of their article so clearly that they can set down a detailed outline and start to write from it. This type of writer can begin at the beginning, move from one topic to the next and fit one paragraph in after another like the pieces of a puzzle, each in its proper place. If he later changes the order, he cuts the material apart, puts it together again following a new plan and rewrites the sentences that connect one topic to the next.

Other writers, after the preliminary sorting, make a first draft of the whole—and this is often an easy way to get started, as the chapter on "Writing and Rewriting" shows—and arrive at the final order in a subsequent draft.

Still others, having decided on the different elements to be covered, write up each topic separately. One excellent writer I know writes up each topic when he is in the mood for it. If the last persons he has interviewed for an article are the educators and he is full of that topic, he tackles that first, finishes it and goes on to whatever next section he is inclined to. When all sections are on paper, he shuffles the sections around and in a later draft finds his final order and writes the connecting sentences. There comes a time when the right order seems inevitable.

Many writers get as far as the final draft before they discover the best lead and conclusion.

Basic principles

Along with the physical pattern of lead, theme, body and conclusion we have been discussing, structure is also built on the three principles of *unity, coherence* and *emphasis.*

A unified article is one in which the writer has always before him the purpose of his piece; he follows that purpose through from beginning to end, and does not allow himself to be led off into by-ways, however attractive they may be. And sometimes it is hard to resist them.

In your portrait of the aspiring Senator, for example, you would include something on his family background only if it had a bearing on his going to college. If he had decided on college as a mark of his rebellion against the illiteracy of his parents, or if he had been urged by his parents to make the effort, references to them would be relevant. If his family had no bearing on his going to college, then a bare mention would be sufficient.

It is easy to speculate on the by-roads Theodore Irwin might have discovered in his research for "Reading Writing." He might have been tempted to include something about the florid penmanship of the last century. He would certainly have remembered the voluminous writings of the Adamses, much of which is still legible. But his piece was not concerned with the past; it is of today, so cross those items off. He would also have heard much from school people about the arguments for and against different styles of writing. But his purpose was not to take up the cudgels for one style versus another. He was interested only in legibility. So that digression was passed up.

If you are tempted to go off on a tangent in your own writing, ask yourself, "Does this apply to my theme?" If it does not, then out with it.

Signals

Coherence is achieved very simply by using transitional sentences or paragraphs as you move from one topic in your piece to the next. These transitions (also called bridges) are the glue that holds an article together. They are also a mark of good manners in the writer. If you are driving a car, when you go from one lane to another or make a turn, you signal your intention to other cars near you. When you move from one topic to another in an article or change your direction, you also warn the reader of your intention. Without these transitions your article is jumpy, and it is hard for the reader to follow your thought.

Often the transition can be made in a few words. If you have presented one side of a controversy and wish to give the opposing argument, you can signal your turn with *but, on the other hand, yet, however,* for instance. If you are adding more incidents to prove your point, you have words such as *also, what's more, again, furthermore.* If you wish to show the result of some action, there is *hence, accordingly, consequently.*

Used often, these connective words make an article sound pedantic and give the impression of a lazy writer.

It is more graceful and more informative to insert a sentence or two or even a whole paragraph to make the transition. Occasionally the last sentence of one paragraph makes the bridge to the first sentence of the next. Turn back to the detailed outline of "Reading Writing" and observe the transitions. And make a point of observing them in the next article you read. Or, for that matter, the next story or novel.

Sometimes you omit the transitions inadvertently. The sequence of events or facts is so clear in your own mind that you think it will be equally clear to the reader. Don't take a chance on it. You have been immersed in your subject for weeks; the reader is coming to it fresh. Failure to signal a turn on a parkway might result in a fatal accident. Omit transitions in an article and the results could be disastrous to your piece; you might lose your reader.

Emphasis

There are a number of ways of giving *emphasis* to an article:

1. Build up one topic or one person and relegate other related topics or people to a secondary position. To illustrate:

A young writer recently wrote a poignant little piece about her experience when she took three children from an orphanage to a beach for a day's outing. There was a small child of three, a bright but hard-boiled little boy of ten, and a shy and rather sullen girl of thirteen. She began by describing all three children; in telling of the drive out she permitted the ten-year-old to monopolize the article; at the beach the three-year-old took over, and yet the climax to the outing came through the thirteen-year-old girl.

She submitted the piece to three magazines, one after the other. In each case, she had first written a query letter, and each of the journals had asked to see the article. Each finally returned it with a cordial letter ("Do let us see something else of yours") telling her that it was charmingly written but "not right for us just now."

After a struggle to find the reason for its rejection, she realized that she had so divided her attention among the three children, that there was not a complete account of any one of them. She rewrote, playing down the two younger children, but keeping the girl in the forefront throughout the day and following her varying moods until they came to a climax at the end.

2. An unqualified statement that goes right to the heart of the discussion often gives *emphasis* to the whole piece. Examples: John F. Kennedy's, "Ask not what your country can do for you; ask what you can do for your country." Or Franklin D. Roosevelt's, "The only thing we have to fear is fear itself." Or Churchill's indomitable, "I have nothing to offer but blood, toil, tears and sweat."

3. The position in which you place your main point can give it *emphasis*. It should be either at the beginning or the end. If at the beginning, then the body of the article is devoted to discussing and proving it; if at the end, the body builds up the discussion and proof and so leads to the final statement. Or you can emphasize your main point by giving it the lion's share of your space.

If all this seems like keeping too many balls in the air at once, don't worry. *Lead, theme, body* and *conclusion* are so obvious you can't forget them. Be sure to remember also the words *unity* (keep your eye on the ball); *coherence* (glue the parts together); and *emphasis* (don't scatter your shots). Check your article against them.

This structure of the magazine article is very different from that of a newspaper piece. The structure of the newspaper piece resembles a kite with a long tail. All the important facts are in the beginning—the kite itself; the details, which in a magazine article would be woven into the body of the piece, are written one after the other in descending importance—the tail. As each succeeding edition of the paper comes out and other news must be included, the editor can chop off the tail, bit by bit, and still have the main facts in the head. The newspaper is usually thrown out each day.

The magazine stays longer on the reading table and each article is planned to be read through to the end. It is an integrated whole.

ℵ 12

THE PROFILE

VOTED MOST POPULAR in almost any poll of editors and readers is the well-written and well-constructed profile —a portrait in words of a person who, for a variety of reasons, is interesting to other people. The name was invented by *The New Yorker* in its first issue of February 21, 1925; fourteen years later in 1939, *The Reader's Digest* launched its version as "My Most Unforgettable Character."

Each of these magazines considered its new series an important contribution to its pages and commissioned outstanding writers to prepare them. The subject of the first *New Yorker* profile was Giulio Gatti-Casazza, at that time general manager of the Metropolitan Opera, and it was written under a pen name by Gilbert Gabriel, a well-known critic. *The Reader's Digest* announced its new feature as "the first of a series being written by famous authors of America and Europe." A. J. Cronin wrote the first "Unforgettable," and among its other early contributors were Stefan Zweig, Sherwood Anderson, Pierre van Paassen, Robert P. Tristram Coffin and André Maurois.

Both of these magazines have since made these "portraits in words" editorial stand-bys. Today, profiles are found in practically every magazine, Sunday supplement, house organ, and newspaper.

Voyage of discovery

The profile may be a quickie—a short piece of a thousand words or less—which devotes itself to only one incident in the subject's life or one facet of his personality. It may be a major study of the person and run from five to ten thousand words. Or, expanded to book length, it may become a biography.

From the writer's side of the fence, the collecting of facts for the portrait and the actual writing are among his most engrossing pursuits. Through his research, he comes to know another person intimately, and that in itself is a voyage of discovery. The writer is a storyteller, but the hero is not dreamed up; he is a real person.

The *short profile* reads so easily, it would seem to be a cinch to write. But it requires its own techniques. Here is an excellent example of just over two hundred words, by Leslie Lieber in *This Week* (June 27, 1965):

PITCHER WHO PAINTS

Jim Bouton of the New York Yankees is the only pitcher in the major leagues who stands a chance to end up in both the Hall of Fame and the Guggenheim Museum of Art. Few people know that Jim Bouton would almost rather paint than pitch. He also is an accomplished sculptor, has molded pottery, and fashions jewelry with such exquisiteness that several top Fifth Avenue firms have offered him jobs.

But Jim's first and abiding artistic love is water colors. He had already studied seriously at Chicago's Art Institute and was taking advanced courses in painting at Western Michigan University when a Yankee scout whisked him away from a life of easels.

Jim's work at school won important scholarships. In fact, several lucky Chicagoans may own Jim Bouton originals without realizing it; in 1957, the budding artist exhibited several paintings in the annual outdoor show on Rush Street. He wanted to sell one or two for enough money to take his fiancée on a Saturday night spree. Instead, he sold them all and got married.

Later this year a top New York gallery plans an exhibit of the Yankee pitcher's latest works.

Does he find it odd to be a pitcher who paints, or a painter who pitches? "No, I just like to work with my hands," he says.

Analysis

As you analyze this little piece, make note of the following:

1. The author limits himself to only one of Mr. Bouton's characteristics—his talent as an artist—and that would come as a surprise to many readers. (Since his subject is nationally known, Mr. Lieber contents himself with merely identifying him as the Yankee pitcher.)

2. In his opening, the author establishes Bouton's dual personality: "Jim Bouton of the New York Yankees is the only pitcher in the major leagues who stands a chance to end up in both the Hall of Fame and the Guggenheim Museum of Art. Few people know that Jim Bouton would almost rather paint than pitch."

3. With his theme thus indicated, he tells us at once of

Bouton's success as an artist, and traces his growth in that field.

4. He builds interest with an amusing anecdote. As a beginner, Bouton had hoped to sell one or two of his paintings in order to take his fiancée out on a date. "He sold them all and got married."

5. He introduces a news note: a New York gallery will shortly give Bouton an exhibition.

6. He ends with the pitcher-artist's own explanation of why he thinks he is succeeding in two fields, "I just like to work with my hands."

Subjects

For your own writing, think of people you know who might furnish similar studies. From my youth in a Kentucky town, I remember Mr. Fritz Grader, the burly German who was our local expressman. When anyone was going traveling, it was Mr. Fritz who came by, hoisted the trunks on his wagon and carted them off to the railroad station. But Mr. Fritz was also a violinist. His strong hands, that dealt so capably with our heavy trunks, showed astonishing delicacy when he reached for his fiddle to play for the high school commencement. Our local paper might have liked the little story.

One summer morning one of my students, looking for profile material, passed a New York garage near which four Good Humor men were loading up to go to Central Park. He stopped to talk with them, made friends, learned how they worked, how much they made, how they chose their stands, and he then wrote an informative piece on what it takes to become a successful Good Humor salesman. Another student wrote of a garage foreman who devoted his weekends to serving as an inspector at stock car races. A company house organ was delighted to have it.

You may know of a Sunday School teacher who has a lively following of teen-agers. One of the religious journals might be interested.

The secret is to open your eyes and look about you. When you find a likely subject, get acquainted—you will find that most people love to talk about themselves. Jot down what you have learned in your notebook. For some of your little stories you may find a market at once; some you will hoard until you need them.

My own writing has been filled with people I knew in Kentucky. I recall my first job in New York as secretary to the managing editor of *Survey Graphic*: As I was typing the manuscript of an article we had accepted about the farm problem, I remembered a poverty-stricken tenant farmer at whose cabin I had stopped one hot Sunday morning to ask the way. The door was open and as I waited for an answer to my knock I could see the unmade beds, the unwashed dishes, the tawdry furnishings and the one proud possession, a parlor organ. When I finally located the farmer, his whole family, down to the three-year-old baby, were out in the hot sun working in the tobacco field. A more down-and-out little group I had never seen. They were bone tired and dispirited.

My editor needed a short human interest blurb for the contents page. He let me try my hand at it and my word picture of that destitute little family illustrated the plight of the sharecropper. It was my first published effort in a national magazine. The editor gave me other short bits to write, and I was on my way to becoming an editor.

Years later when I was on *McCall's*, we were looking

for a human interest feature and I remembered Mrs. Josephus Martin (Mrs. Doctor Martin, we called her) who was famous for her angel food cakes. No wedding or birthday was complete without one. Carefully set in a hatbox and packed in tissue paper, one of Mrs. Martin's cakes was the great present from home to the boy or girl at college. I realized that every town and neighborhood had some woman famous for a food specialty. And Mrs. Martin became the inspiration for a series of short profiles which we called "The Best Cook in Our Town."

The *longer profile* gives a more complete picture of its subject. The short profile is like a quick drawing; the longer one becomes a portrait in oils. It requires more research, a deeper insight into the subject's character, and skill in building up the various elements of your picture.

If you are a beginning writer, I suggest that you begin with the short sketch and move on to the rounded portrait as your skill increases.

To illustrate the more complete portrait, here is Sam Shumate's "The Most Unforgettable Character I've Met" (*Reader's Digest,* September, 1962):

THE MOST UNFORGETTABLE CHARACTER I'VE MET

by Sam Shumate

He was so short and skinny that, when you saw him trudging through the passes of our mile-high Blue Ridge Mountains, he looked like just a little something stuffed into the tops of his flapping rubber boots. Yet Oddie Cox, principal of the Ashe County school for Negroes, at Bristol, N.C., was one of the biggest and wisest persons I've known.

Mr. Oddie, as we whites called him (the Negroes called him Professor), entered my life about ten years ago, on a spring morning shortly after my 14th birthday. I was down by the creek in the backyard when my grandmother, with whom I lived, called, "Son, there's someone here to see you."

I ran around the house and found myself facing the first Negro I'd ever seen close up. (Our village of Warrensville is in a secluded pocket of the Appalachians where the Negro population is small.) There, smiling, stood a little man in his 60's whose head seemed too large for his spindly frame. He extended a hand and, in a voice as gentle as music, introduced himself and said, "I am taking some of your friends camping this weekend. I wonder if you would like to join us."

Astonished, I looked at my grandmother. She smiled and nodded. "It'll be all right, son, if Mr. Oddie's going to take you." I was to learn that most parents felt that way. A youngster was bound to be all right if Oddie Cox was looking after him.

Mr. Oddie was a master woodsman. He showed us how to make a fire without matches. He showed us how to cook without utensils, devise crow-callers from split laurel twigs and make fine fishing poles from hickory saplings.

"The trout in these pools," he told us in his precise, professor-like way, "will best strike flies made of bright-colored feathers. But where will we get such feathers?" When we gave up on the problem, Mr. Oddie sprinkled some bread crumbs on the ground and, hiding near them, began to whistle shrilly. Presently some redbirds alighted on the crumbs and started fighting over them. Mr. Oddie picked up three or four feathers they knocked out of one another. "Well!" he said, as if surprised. "It seems our friends have provided us with our trout flies."

The thing that impressed me most about Mr. Oddie was his *method* of teaching. Time and again he would just wonder out loud. "I wonder," he would say, "how long this river's been running by here. I wonder what all this old river has seen . . . what it could tell us about all the ages of men who have walked its banks and dreamed their dreams." Mr. Oddie wondered about things in such an intriguing way that you found yourself wondering about them, too—and wanting to know the answers to questions it had never occurred to you to ask before.

Though I didn't see Mr. Oddie again for a year, I learned a lot more about him. The grandson of slaves, Oddie Cox had been born in a shack near the site of his present school. His mother had given him his name in the hope that he'd turn out to be something "odd"—special—and he certainly had. At 18, in a one-room mockery of a school of the kind he had attended himself, Oddie had become a teacher of the isolated mountain children of his race.

There were practically no roads then in our region. So that his children could get to school in winter, "Professor Cox" would plow paths through the thigh-deep snowdrifts with a scrape made of boards and drawn by a mule. Years later, with his own money, he bought the county's first "school bus" for Negroes—an old green panel truck that he converted into a bus himself. Now, at 63, he drove a modern bus furnished by the county, and had a "big," comfortable, four-room, consolidated school under his principalship. Best of all, the two teachers who helped him with his 50-odd pupils both had master's degrees.

I learned that on weekends, if one or two pupils wanted to "study ahead" of the rest, Mr. Oddie would help them at home. And to keep "studying ahead" himself, he spent his summers down at the Agricultural and Technical College (A & T) at Greensboro. How he had time to give further help to boys of other schools in a dozen mountain villages, I'll never know—but he did.

The spring following our first camping trip I was bitten by a copperhead while playing baseball. Mr. Oddie walked 17 miles to see me and bring me a pint of my favorite ice cream, butter pecan. "Well, Sammy," he said to cheer me up, "is it true that the snake that bit you died?" In the weeks that followed, he came often. It was because my parents were separated and living elsewhere, I think, that he decided to give me so much attention.

I'd never talked to anyone who knew so much about so many things. He was the first to make history and algebra come alive for me. He aroused my interest in good music. He was the first to tell me that the Blue Ridge, though beautiful, was a "depressed area" of shut-down mines and starving farms —a place from which young people should try to "reach out."

How did Mr. Oddie know so much about music? I found that in his mid-60's he had begun to try to strengthen his whispery-weak voice and teach himself piano and musical composition—this to improve the quality of music at the daily devotionals held at his school. He learned to play and sing so well that he became the regular pianist at his church and a favorite soloist at the white church at Nathan's Creek.

"There is so much to learn, Sammy," he'd say, almost regretfully. "Never miss a chance to learn anything you can!"

One day when I was a senior in high school, as we sat under the cottonwood tree that stands in the center of the little dusty crossroads in front of my grandmother's house, Mr. Oddie mused, "I wonder where all these roads go."

"Well," I said, "one goes south to Boone, North Carolina; one goes west to Mountain City, Tennessee; and one goes north to Marion, Virginia."

"Ah," said Mr. Oddie, "but don't all roads lead to other roads?" He took out a worn map of the world, and unfolded it on the bench between us. "This is your world now," he said, making a pencil dot at Warrensville. "But you and your world have got to grow, haven't you?" On the map he drew a series of larger and larger circles that stretched out like ripples in a pool. "You see," he said, laying his pencil on the map to make a wheel-spoke extending from the hub of our crossroads, "the road to Boone can also lead to Caracas or Buenos Aires. The road to Tennessee can lead to Shanghai or Tokyo."

"And have you been to these places?" I asked naïvely.

"Oh, no." He chuckled at the thought. "But you are young. Study and enlarge yourself enough and you may see them all!"

But college seemed financially impossible for me, and I was sick of school anyway. Some of my friends had gotten factory jobs in the valley, and already they had new cars and spending money. Urgently wanting these things, too, I let it be known, as my graduation approached, that I'd take the first job that came along. Then one morning there stood Mr. Oddie on our front porch, as close to anger as I'd ever seen him.

"I understand," he said, "that you are going to sell your future for an automobile. I wonder if a car can ever take you far enough that the men who learn more won't pass you one day."

"But that's just it!" I blurted. "I want to get out of these Godforsaken mountains. I want to get out where there's *real* work to do!"

"Certainly," Mr. Oddie said quietly. "But how far did you say you were going? To the nearest factory? Filling station? To *here*, Sam?"

To my astonishment, he whipped out the map on which he had drawn the expanding circles. His pencil went tap-tap-tap on the close-by valley towns in which I was hoping for a job. They were all within the first small circle centered by the dot called Warrensville.

"It's clear you're not ready in your mind for college yet," he said. "But, Sam"—his pencil continued to tap in the tiny center circle—"is *this* as far as you want to go, as much as you want to see?"

Mr. Oddie rose abruptly. "I hear you're a very good mechanic," he said. "I wonder if you have ever considered this." As he left, he slipped a bright-colored folder into my hand. It said, "Join the United States Air Force and Learn a Profession." The profession he had underlined was aircraft mechanic.

When I left Warrensville for basic training in San Antonio, Mr. Oddie was there to see me off, standing quietly in the background as if all he wanted was to get in a little good-by wave. After I got through the school for jet mechanics and began flying all over the globe—Iceland, Norway, Denmark, Germany, Hawaii, Japan, Formosa—I still received a letter from Mr. Oddie regularly, once a month. He knew more about the countries I visited than I did, and he made suggestions of things to see and do and ponder.

After I returned home from my Air Force tour of duty, I went down to Mr. Oddie's neat little house at Nathan's Creek. I found him reading one of his two worn encyclopedias. He looked old and tired as he squinted up through rimless glasses to see who had stepped in the door. "Sammy!" he said, recognizing me. Then, pulling up a chair for me, "Well, Sammy, how did you enjoy the world?"

"It was fine, Mr. Oddie," I said. "But I'm glad to be back."

He sat beaming at me delightedly. "And so now you're ready to settle down and go to college—and right in our mountains, too, they tell me! You know something?" He chuckled. "That's what I always sort of thought you'd do."

That was the last time I ever saw Mr. Oddie. I began working my way through Appalachian State Teachers College at Boone, 25 miles down the Ridge. The night before I came home for spring holiday, Mr. Oddie's house burned to the ground. His body was found in the ashes.

The Oddie Cox funeral was unlike any other I've ever attended. For half a mile, both sides of the red clay road winding up the hill were lined with cars. As I climbed the lane, I saw license plates from New York, Michigan, Colorado, California—vivid reminders of how widely Mr. Oddie's "children" had gotten around. Two white ministers assisted the Negro pastor in conducting the service. Three white men and three Negroes were pallbearers. It was a time for plain words spoken from the heart. One minister put it: "Little has to be said for Mr. Oddie, for his actions spoke for him. His life was an open book, and anyone was welcome to read it."

A few weeks after the funeral something happened that made me wonder if we whom Oddie Cox had known so well really had known *him* well at all. Oddie's sister, Rene, received through the mail a bachelor-of-science degree—Mr. Oddie's first. It came from A & T, and it was conferred as of eight months before Mr. Oddie's death. Astonished (I'd always assumed he'd had a degree—perhaps even several degrees—for many years), I went down to A & T and looked up the record of student Oddie James Cox. It was a pathetic but thrilling revelation.

Mr. Oddie had started as a freshman at the age of 46. Continuing for 23 summers, he had taken on one of the darnedest hodgepodges of courses (87 of them in all) ever attempted by a student of the college. First he had tackled spelling, writing and arithmetic (things his mountain school had failed to teach him well as a child); then he went on to courses like scouting and coaching, and finally to subjects like geography, biology, botany, chemistry, history and child psychology.

"You see," explained A & T's acting president Lewis C. Dowdy, "Oddie Cox was always trying to learn so many things at once that none of them added up to a degree in any one field. His grades were not the best, either. He chose the subjects he knew the least about, and naturally these were the hardest for him. But Mr. Cox wasn't particularly interested in amassing credits for himself. What he was interested in was learning everything he could so he could teach it to those children up there where he lived."

"I know," I said.

"Last summer," President Dowdy said, "we decided to give Oddie his degree on the basis of what he had *accomplished*. He said he'd rather wait until next June to receive his diploma formally, in cap and gown and all. He said he had some friends in the mountains he'd like to bring down to see him get it. But then, of course, there was that fire. . . ."

Up in our mountains, some of the white and Negro leaders got together to build a little memorial to Mr. Oddie. They bought the best wire fencing the hardware store carries, and the best locust posts. They put up a fine fence around the churchyard where he lies, and on the gate there is a brass plaque reading: "In Loving Memory of Oddie J. Cox."

As for me, I'm not leaving. There are, after all, still some pretty big opportunities here on the Blue Ridge to "reach out" —especially for teachers. I'm going to be a teacher here. I wonder if Mr. Oddie wouldn't have liked that.

Analysis

As you study the above and other profiles from today's magazines, you will discover some rather well-defined guidelines that writers follow. Check your own conclusions with these:

1. Know as much about your subject as possible. Read what has been published about him; interview people who know him—those who admire him and those who don't;

and talk with him personally. Collect much more information about him than you will use, to get a clear picture of his life, from his childhood on, and perhaps something about his parents.

Mr. Shumate wrote his piece largely from his own memory of Mr. Oddie, and Mr. Oddie probably told him much about his early life and parents, but when he came to write, the author undoubtedly talked with the neighbors who had known Mr. Oddie in his youth, and he went to the Agricultural and Technical College to find the record of Mr. Oddie's career as a student.

2. Focus on some special aspect of his life or character for your story. Even in a longer profile, you can't hope to do a complete biography, so make a selection from all your material that will establish the theme of your own piece; then include only those side incidents that round out your picture.

Mr. Shumate's article is focused on Mr. Oddie's passion for learning and his gift for passing it along to his pupils.

3. Arrive at your own opinion of your hero. If you find him in some ways admirable and in others less admirable and plan to include both, indicate that from the beginning. Don't show him as a paragon of virtue for the first two-thirds of your piece and then make him a blackguard at the end. You are not writing a mystery story.

Mr. Shumate had only love for Mr. Oddie, but he shows him to us as a funny-looking little man, and we learn that he didn't do too well in his college work because he couldn't resist taking too many subjects.

4. Collect lots of anecdotes about him; specific stories bring your subject to life, and are worth pages of generalities.

5. Take notes to show the flavor of his speech and include dialogue.

6. Write a lead that will give the reader some reason for caring about your hero or about that aspect of his life which you plan to stress. An opening anecdote or statement that gives a quick picture of the subject, *plus* a statement to arouse the curiosity of the reader, is an almost sure-fire formula. But there are many kinds of successful leads. Study other profiles for examples of successful leads.

Mr. Shumate begins with a quick picture of a short, skinny, odd-looking little man, then in the next sentence promises a surprise: "Yet Oddie Cox, principal of the Ashe County school for Negroes, at Bristol, N.C., was one of the biggest and wisest persons I've known."

7. At some point in your piece, answer the big question of how your hero became the person he is. Are there hints for the reader in the account of his career? Does your article clear up any possible speculation about the subject in the reader's mind? Has he an inspirational or heroic quality that gives the reader an awareness of a good life?

Mr. Shumate's article answers the last question.

8. Let your conclusion give a summary of your own evaluation of your subject, and, if possible, tie the ending to the lead.

In telling of the collaboration of the white and Negro neighbors on a memorial fence and plaque, the author shows their feelings toward the hero.

9. Leave the reader with a last incident that is memorable. Depending on the tone and purpose of your piece, make it tender, inspirational, critical or amusing.

In his last paragraph we learn of Mr. Oddie's influence on the author's life. It is both tender and inspirational.

"As for me, I'm not leaving. There are, after all, still some pretty big opportunities here on the Blue Ridge to 'reach out'—especially for teachers. I'm going to be a teacher here. I wonder if Mr. Oddie wouldn't have liked that."

10. Finally, keep in mind that you are dealing with facts, and you must be able to back up any statement you make.

As you read some profile you especially like, observe how the writer has covered these points. Read as a professional does, and what you learn will improve your own facility as a writer.

א 13

THE "I" PIECE—PERSONAL EXPERIENCE ARTICLES AND THE ESSAY

PERHAPS THE MOST tempting article for the writer is the personal experience piece. It would seem to be as easy as writing a letter; often it requires neither library research nor interviewing. All you have to do is reach back into your memory and come out with a piece.

And the publications are eager for these articles. *Reader's Digest* offers $2500 for "an hitherto unpublished narrative of an unusual personal experience"; *Redbook* offers $500 for a young mother's story; *McCall's* offers $1000 for the story of a turning-point in your life; and the contents page of almost all popular journals lists one or more first person articles. Here are some titles from a single issue of some of our mass-circulation periodicals:

Saturday Evening Post
> *Keep Out of My Kid's Hair* by Bruce Jay Friedman (Father's protest to school which would cut his son's long locks)

My Life in a Soviet Prison by Peter Landerman
Ladies' Home Journal

My Second Family by Bing Crosby
I Just Stepped out of Vogue by Jean Kerr (Humor)
Reader's Digest

    Guardian Angel of the Air Well by Robert Hamilton (A story of how the author and his wife soothed an angry child)

    Alone against the Sea by William Willis, condensed from the *Saturday Evening Post* (Adventure)

    Incident at the Soda Fountain by Louise Lee Outlaw, condensed from *Philadelphia Sunday Bulletin Magazine* (How a parent handled a thieving youth in the presence of his children)

    You Take Progress, I'll Take Tooth Powder by James Lincoln Collier, condensed from *Contemporary* (Amusing reminiscence)

McCall's

    A Very Easy Death by Simone de Beauvoir (Story of her mother's death and her reaction to it)

    Why Mommy Can't Read by Jean Kerr (Humor)

Redbook

    I Don't Know Where to Look for Me by Anne Taylor (The frustrations of an ostensibly happy young woman)

    The Feather of a Dove by Barney Crile (A husband's story of a happy marriage with a tribute to his wife)

    Florida's Gulf Coast by William B. Hartley (Account of a journey by author and his family)

Good Housekeeping

    My Problem: Tragic Pregnancy, Anonymous (German measles)

It Was a Beautiful Wedding, but . . . by Janet McGregor (The cost of a big wedding as told by the bride)

As you see from the above, personal experience articles may be on many subjects. Here is a quick rundown of the general classifications which are most popular:

1. *The family article.* Women's magazines are especially fond of these—some publish them monthly in a continuing series; they are also popular with grocery store journals, Sunday newspaper supplements, religious family magazines, some of the fraternal magazines, etc.

They are likely to deal with teen-agers, bachelors, spinsters, career women, but more often with husbands and wives, their relations with each other, their children, in-laws, etc. The author gives a first-person account of a situation he had had to face and how he worked it out. *The Catholic Layman* published a husband's story, "How to Save Your Wife's Sanity." A surprising point of view or a new slant on an old subject is salable: "In "We Decided to Stay Poor," for instance, a wife tells that they preferred not to risk the husband's health by having him strive for a more ambitious job.

Many are of parents' problems with their children. For example, "How We Solved the TV Problem"; or a mother's story of how she struggled to keep a mentally defective child, although she was sapping her strength and depriving her other children. Along the same line is the "I Disagree" piece, in which the writer doesn't cotton to some prevailing notion. After *McCall's* put forth its "togetherness" program, there came a rash of articles in other journals on "We Want More Apartness" and "I Don't Want to be a Pal to my Son." When any new idea in child rearing or education comes along, the for and against pieces inevitably follow.

2. *The disability piece* is about someone disabled and tells how he or she adjusts to the disability and makes a good life in spite of it.

3. *The helpful hints and how-to pieces*—"How We Laid our Flagstone Terrace," "How I Overcame my Slice in Golf," etc. etc. Just keep in mind that your idea must be workable and, if possible, new. If you are telling how you remodeled your living room, your possibilities of a sale will be increased if you have *before* and *after* pictures, or "before" pictures in any event. The publication will often take its own "after" shots.

4. *Travel articles* told in the first person. For examples, see almost any issue of *Holiday, Travel, Venture, Ford Times,* etc.

5. *Personal adventure narratives* are very popular in men's and sports publications.

6. *Ghostwritten articles.* "My Husband, Jack Celebrity," as told to Marian Writer would have been actually written by Miss Writer, but told as if Mrs. Celebrity had composed it.

Guidelines

Now for some guidelines on writing the personal experience piece:

1. It must be sincere. If it seems phonied up, it is no good. Even if you have borrowed some incidents to build your piece, they must be incidents that could have happened under those circumstances, and they must sound true. To illustrate: One of my students wrote an account of his experiences sailing a very small boat from New Jer-

sey to Bermuda with his fifteen-year-old daughter and a
friend. He planned to submit the article to one of the
yachting magazines. He had made the same trip the year
before with the same crew and had acquired some techniques that would be of use to other small boat sailors—
a way of stowing canned goods, for instance, so that even
as they were used up, the boat remained in balance.

There was a spirited account of a squall; the piece was
adequate without much sparkle. His previous trip had
been his daughter's initiation into distance sailing and
her reaction had been original and amusing. When he
brought these forward into the account of the second trip,
the piece took on a fresh and lively pace.

2. The structure of the personal experience piece must
be as solid as that of any other article. It must not just
meander off into gossip. The lead and subsequent paragraphs must introduce the characters and set up the problem; the body of the article must build the story, and the
conclusion should suggest a solution.

Let's look at what might be the structure of a disability
article about a woman who has been stricken by polio. It
might open with her discovery, in the hospital, of her
helplessness. For the theme it might flash back to her comfortable home before her illness, with her husband and
three children, including a thirteen-year-old daughter,
who is just beginning to grow up. (This daughter is to be
the center of her problem.) Next, perhaps, her return
home, her frustrations as she tries to take up again the
reins of her household, and her discovery that her daughter seems to be completely out of hand. Then follows an
account of her small successes in handling her physical
disabilities; her continuing worry over her daughter; her

inability to attend parent-teacher meetings; the difficulty of arranging small parties at home for her child; and finally, the incident or event that brings her daughter back into the heart of the family.

3. The subject must be one that is of interest to many people. As we read a well-written personal experience article, we should be able to put ourselves in the writer's place. The rather trite outline above of the disabled mother has at least two points of interest: every mother's fear of what would happen to her family if she were crippled and unable to function; and her desire to guide and keep the confidence of her growing children.

If the first-person articles are humorous—and they frequently are—we get a double enjoyment if we compare them with our own similar ludicrous experiences.

4. The writer must tell his story from an objective point of view. And here lies the greatest pitfall.

To avoid it, remember that the most interesting person to you is yourself, so you enjoy writing about yourself. But the most important person to the reader is *himself,* so your personal experience must reach him and illuminate his life, or he stops reading. To put it bluntly, you must break out of the emotional bonds that tie you to your experience, look at it from the outside, and ask yourself, "What will this give the reader?" Once you have been able to take yourself outside your experience and look at it from a little distance, you are well on the way to writing a piece that will awake a response in the reader, and that is what the editor is looking for.

But this is easier said than done, especially if you are writing of an experience that has deeply affected you. A subject dear to many writers is their own childhood, and in these Freudian days, the trend is to tell of the rebuffs suffered at the hands of crass associates or unfeeling adults. Adolescent pains and marital difficulties are also in demand. These are all legitimate subjects if you can avoid falling into self-pity on the one hand or self-glorification on the other. You are likely to tell the world either, "See what a hard time I had," or "Look at how brave I was." Ten to one the editor says, "Ah, me," and sends the articles back.

A young writer I know had collected a variety of rejection slips on stories of children, all slightly fictionized accounts of unhappy incidents of her own childhood. Finally, convinced that editors were insensitive to childhood sufferings, she put them away. A year or so later when she read them over, her own verdict was, "I certainly was feeling sorry for myself when I wrote those."

And at the same time, some of the most poignant and eloquent plays, novels and articles are about the writers' own experiences. The authors of these were in control of their emotions and not ridden by them.

Another caution: Don't try to make a personal experience article pay off old scores.

An elderly woman who had worked all her life and was now approaching retirement with little savings felt she had been cheated out of a pension by an organization she had once worked for, and undertook to tell the world about this injustice through an article. Her outrage and resentment produced merely a wail of hard luck. She was so mired in her woes that she became unable to do the research to discover whether her problem was an isolated one or of enough general interest to attract a number of readers: It was unsalable.

Other favorite subjects are our own relatives. "My Aunt Em was certainly a type," we tell ourselves and undertake to make an unforgettable character out of her. Here again our emotions can play us false. We tend to see our relatives either in the rosy glow of affection, so they come through our prose like blobs of jelly, or as objects of such deep-seated resentments that we can't avoid taking jabs at them. In other words, we are likely to be writing for our own comfort or satisfaction and not for our readers.

Although these personal whines and resentments are not likely to be accepted and published, I would not for anything dissuade you from writing them. For one thing, you get them out of your system and once your mind is clear of them, you are free to go on to more objective writing.

Also, in the writing you may have captured an emotion or description of a state of mind that will serve you well in another setting. In other words, these items really belong in your notebook. Once when I needed to recapture a southern spring, I found it in my notebook in a description of the young leaves on sycamores along a swollen, muddy creek. Again, in writing about an adolescent school dropout, I found what I needed in a little story of my own heartache and rejection as a high school girl.

A third advantage comes from the fact that you write these personal outpourings with a sense of urgency. If you are writing of yourself, you try to capture the exact emotion; if you are writing of a relative you know well, you work to recreate your picture of that person in words. And these are skills you will need time and again.

But when the personal experience is well done, it is superb: Remember James Thurber's *The Night the Bed Fell Down* and his other Columbus, Ohio, pieces; Clar-

ence Day's *Life with Father* went on and on for weeks
and months and years; made its way to the stage and
screen and is still being enjoyed. Nora Johnson recaptured
her adolescent experiences in a story for *The New Yorker,*
later made into the movie, *The World of Henry Orient.*

The essay

The brief space given here to the essay corresponds
roughly to the space this neglected form of non-fiction
receives in our periodicals today. I would like to see it
given more, for what is called the "familiar essay" seems
to me delightful reading. I do not mean the formal ex-
pository essay such as So-and-So's "Essay on the Theory of
Style," but rather the genial and sometimes gently ironic
ruminations of a thoughtful writer, addressed to readers
who share his values and with whom he is congenial, completely relaxed and at ease.

Although there are practically no rules for this kind of
composition—the writer follows his own humor and is
free to wander into whatever side roads his mood dictates
—the essay is probably the only form of literature which
was invented on a certain day and by a certain person:
Michel de Montaigne, a 38-year-old French nobleman who
left public life in March of 1571 and retired to his country
house to devote his life to writing.

His subject was himself. "Because I found I had nothing
else to write about, I presented myself as a subject." He
gave his works the name of "essays," which meant that
these were experiments in a new kind of literature. "It is
the only book of its kind in the world," he said. "It is so
fantastic and extraordinary that perhaps it will pass. . . .
Custom has made it a fault to speak of oneself . . . in

hatred of the boasting which always seems to attach itself to self-testimony."

Not only did the essay not pass, but it has been handed down by a long line of writers including Charles Lamb, Henry David Thoreau, Ralph Waldo Emerson, R. L. Stevenson, and in our own century by Max Beerbohm, G. K. Chesterton, Mark Twain, Robert Benchley and Joseph Wood Krutch. Mr. Krutch's essays, written over a period of several years, have been collected into a book, *If You Don't Mind My Saying So—*, a title which also defines this form of writing.

Not many essays are to be found in our periodicals today. And I cannot recommend that a writer devote himself to this form of writing with hope of financial reward. I do recommend that for your own enjoyment you read the classic examples of the form from the past—and the present—with attention to the clarity and beauty of the language. And write essays occasionally for the satisfaction you will get from self-expression.

In the stampede today for facts, for information, for culture and for advancement, we have passed up the more leisurely refreshment of the familiar essay. You will find it occasionally in *The Saturday Review, Harper's, The Atlantic, The Nation,* the book review sections of some Sunday papers, *The Reporter,* the first page of the second section of *The Christian Science Monitor* and in some other publications which preserve a tone of intimacy with their readers.

When I said that there were few rules for the essay, I did not mean that this is a formless type of writing. When the author begins his piece, he knows where he will end. He takes the scenic route rather than the throughway, but he comes out at his destination. The following short essay by Ben Hibbs, from *The Reader's Digest* (November, 1964) is a case in point. The writer states his objective when he quotes the lady, "Oh, my *dear* young man, what a *limited* boyhood you must have had!" He reaches his goal in the last paragraph!

BOYHOOD ON THE PRAIRIE

by Ben Hibbs

Not long after I had migrated to the East from my native Kansas, I was invited to a social function in one of Philadelphia's suburbs. During the evening I was introduced to a college professor, a lady who, I learned later, spent her summers in Europe and had never been west of the Alleghenies. Noting my midwestern accent, she asked where I was from.

"From Kansas," I said. "I grew up in Pretty Prairie, Reno County"—and I added as a prudent afterthought, "U.S.A."

"And how large is Pretty Prairie?"

"Well," I replied, "last time I was there, the population was 483; but three young couples were expecting, so it may well be larger now."

The lady placed a sympathetic hand on my arm and said, "Oh, my *dear* young man, what a *limited* boyhood you must have had!"

This was a new and astonishing thought for me, but after I had recovered I spoke to her approximately thus: "Limited boyhood? Why, lady, by the time I was 12 years old, I had heard William Jennings Bryan speak twice at summer chautauqua. I had listened likewise to the Swiss Bell Ringers, who also yodeled. Moreover, at the state fair at Hutchinson, I once saw the fattest hog ever raised in Kansas; he weighed 942 pounds and couldn't get to his feet without the help of a block and tackle. On another occasion, I was actually present when a traveling medicine man demonstrated the strength of his liniment by pouring it right through a solid pine plank. . . ."

I was ready to continue listing the cultural advantages of my youth, but by this time the lady professor had a look of frozen horror on her face. She turned away and began to talk rapidly with another guest about the theories of Sigmund Freud.

Now that my smart-aleck days are past, I wish I had spoken to the lady a little more seriously about my fortunate boyhood in the small-town America which existed shortly after the turn of the century.

I might have told her about the comforts of a home in which there were always plenty of books and magazines and instructive conversation; about parents who believed in what was right and decent, and in giving their children a good education; about a little town where people put their roots down deep into the soil of an America they loved—a town where it wasn't considered nosy to be interested in your neighbors and concerned about them in their time of trouble.

I might have mentioned also the long dusty roads along which a boy could ride his bicycle out to the banks of lazy little creeks, to catch sun perch and bullheads and swim in the buff; the miles upon miles of buffalo grass and rippling wheat fields under the immense prairie sky; the jackrabbits to be hunted, and occasionally the yapping of a coyote in the night; the pageantry of the harvest, with the sweating men, the horse-drawn headers and the great steam threshing rigs clanking down Main Street on their way out to the endless stacks of yellow grain; the covered wagons that were still coming through in ones and twos and threes, carrying people—we called them movers—seeking, as mankind eternally will, a better life somewhere . . . on, somewhere.

And sometimes on a snug winter's evening, a boy could listen to the yarns of the old sodbusters as they sat around the stove in his father's hardware store. Among them were men of foreign extraction. Some were veterans of the Civil War; some had fought, even later, in the final Indian wars. Doubtless there was an element of fiction in the tales they told, but there was also pride. For these were the leathery pioneers who had lived through drought and blizzard and the devastation of the grasshopper years, and who had taken this raw plains country by the scruff of its neck and turned it into a gracious, smiling land.

In those days our public orators called America "the land of opportunity" and "the greatest country on earth," and we never doubted them. In our schools and churches and homes we were taught pride in our country. The copybook maxims dealing with such things as hard work and honesty and patriotism were not only drilled into us; they were believed in and acted upon.

It never occurred to anyone that our environment was limited, or that all this was unsophisticated or corny. It was merely part of the atmosphere of a simpler time and place, when the values of life seemed more nearly black and white. If our attitudes were uncomplicated, they at least strengthened character and put purpose into toil and struggle.

These, then, were some of the facets of a small-town boyhood I should have mentioned to the lady at the party. And I should also have told her this, surely: that in the late afternoon of many crisp autumn days the whole western quadrant of the Kansas heavens, from earth to zenith, flamed with such majesty that some dim comprehension of the Infinite entered even into the heart of a young lad.

Some scientists have said that the brilliance of Kansas sunsets is caused by dust in the air, but this drab explanation seems to me unworthy and untenable. The Lord gave sunsets to the western prairies for the same reason that He gave the rolling Atlantic surf to the eastern seaboard, a noble blaze of fall foliage to New England and snowy mountain peaks to the far West—as therapy for the often troubled human spirit.

Limited youth, indeed!

And now . . . times change, the nation grows urban, life becomes steadily more complex. And who is to say that one era is better than another? Certainly the young today have advantages undreamed of a couple of generations ago, but in the days when America was essentially rural there was a tang in the morning air and dew on the grass, and a far horizon, and these were good for the soul of a boy, and a nation.

Besides the essay, Montaigne left another legacy to writers. He introduced the word "I" into literature, and its use has grown until today it has invaded almost every form of prose and even some poetry. Many novice writers hesitate to go into the first person, fearing, with Montaigne, that it would seem boastful. Don't hold back. Use "I" naturally and without self-consciousness wherever it fits.

Don't be didactic and professorial, though, and don't look down your nose at your reader. To avoid these pitfalls, many writers, in speaking of themselves, employ a slightly self-deprecatory tone. This softens the force of the omnipresent "I," and a confession of one's own short-comings makes for a we're-all-in-the-same-boat rapport with the reader.

For instance, when I was advising you to read some of the classical essays, I might have inserted a sentence like this: "I must confess that although I can spend a pleasant evening with Montaigne and Lamb and Mark Twain,

R. L. Stevenson bores me into ill-humor." This is true and its purpose in this chapter would have been to assure you that you will not lack taste in my eyes if you find some of the oldsters not to your liking either.

Not so long ago what was called the "editorial we" was often used in place of "I." This is now considered old-fashioned, and you should use "we" only when you are referring to two or more persons. Notice Churchill's proper use of both in his *Blood, Toil, Tears, and Sweat* speech. "I have, myself, full confidence that if all do their duty . . . we shall prove ourselves once again able to defend our island home. . . ." The "I" refers to himself, the "we" to the British people.

ༀ 14

THE FACTUAL ARTICLE
AND THE THINK PIECE

THERE IS STILL a place, even in the large-circulation magazines, for the straight factual article which does not depend on personalities to win readers. It does, however, need the following:

1. A subject of interest to a large audience
2. A title and lead that tell at once what the piece is about and what the reader can hope to gain from it
3. A logical structure that builds and enlarges on the subject
4. Transitions that lead from one point of the article to the next
5. A conclusion that sums up the message
6. A clear and interesting style of writing that conveys the author's enthusiasm for his subject and his interest in it
7. The use of words that are comprehensible to the

reader; if scientific or technical terms are used there should be a clear definition of them in layman's language

The following short piece by J. D. Ratcliff from the *Reader's Digest* (November, 1964), is an excellent illustration of the straight factual article. A longer or more complex article would follow the same general plan.

CHOLESTEROL: GUILTY OR NOT GUILTY?

The case is not yet proved, and the defense now offers new evidence—in what may well be medicine's most important mystery

By J. D. Ratcliff

The most sharply debated question in medicine today is this: Is cholesterol circulating in the blood the chief culprit in heart disease—which kills more Americans than all other sicknesses combined? Also, by shifting from high-cholesterol foods (cream, meat, eggs) to polyunsaturated fats (soy, corn and other vegetable oils), can we hope to escape this wrath?

Confusion and disagreement reign. On the one hand Dr. Ancel Keys, well-known physiologist of the University of Minnesota, sees the dietary shift as filled with promise. But Dr. Edward H. Ahrens, Jr., of the Rockefeller Institute has doubts: "There is virtually no evidence that reducing the cholesterol in the diet will reduce the incidence of heart disease."

Confronted with such opposite views, the layman can only take a seat in the jury box and examine the evidence on which cholesterol has been indicted.

Pure cholesterol is white, powdery. Combined with fats and deposited in arteries, it looks waxy, yellowish. It is present in every cell of the body. Particularly rich in it are the brain, spinal cord and nerves—it makes up ten percent of the brain's weight. The commonest gallstones are largely cholesterol. It is a raw material used by the body for production of vitamin D, sex hormones and bile salts. Even if cholesterol is completely eliminated from the diet, the substance continues to circulate in the blood—manufactured mainly by the liver. Its very omnipresence suggests that cholesterol isn't completely villainous.

It becomes the enemy of the human race when it accumulates in the walls of arteries, particularly the coronary arteries that nourish the heart. As deposits grow they are invaded by fibrous material. The artery wall roughens, and blood clots often form at the point of injury. Finally the artery may be blocked completely. When this happens in the heart arteries, there is a heart attack. When it happens in the brain, there is apoplexy.

In 1913 a Russian researcher named Anitschkow fed rabbits cholesterol-rich diets. The fatty deposits produced in their arteries resembled those found in coronary arteries of people who had died of heart attacks. This observation triggered worldwide research into all fats that circulate in the blood—triglycerides, phospholipids, fatty acids, etc. But cholesterol got most attention, in part because an easily performed test was available to check cholesterol levels of blood.

The tens of thousands of blood tests run were in general agreement on one point. In countries where large amounts of animal fats were consumed, blood cholesterol levels were high—and so were heart-disease deaths. The reverse was also true. In Japan, for example, people subsist largely on a low-cholesterol rice-and-fish diet and have only a tenth the heart disease found in the United States. Yet, when Japanese migrate to California and begin consuming the cholesterol-rich U.S. diet, heart-disease rates soar.

A similar situation exists in southern Italy. There, the

diet is mainly vegetable oil, starch and fruit, with little saturated fat,* and there is only a third as much heart disease as in the United States. In general, U.S. citizens derive over 40 percent of their dietary calories from fats. In large parts of Asia, Africa and South America, people consume only a third as much fat, and there heart disease is relatively unimportant.

A continuing study of heart disease in Framingham, Mass., turned up other facts. People who had 244 or more milligrams of cholesterol per 100 c.c of blood had a heart-attack rate three times that of people who had a level under 210 milligrams.

These and similar studies *seemed* to clinch the case: a diet rich in meat and dairy fats hoisted blood levels of cholesterol, paved the way for heart attacks. The case against cholesterol looked black indeed. And, meanwhile, other evidence indicated that switching from dairy products to vegetable oils would reduce blood cholesterol levels—by about 20 percent. Many people concluded that here was an easy means of avoiding heart attack. Food processors rushed in to promote polyunsaturated vegetable oils; some people began avoiding butter and cream. One survey showed that 22 percent of American families modified diets to some extent.

Cautious research men weren't ready for such a leap. Too many unanswered questions remained. Why, for example, did pre-menopausal women have only a fraction the heart disease of their husbands, although both had essentially the same diet? And why did cholesterol levels soar during pregnancy, a time when heart troubles are at a minimum?

Dozens of studies produced conflicting evidence. For example, Dr. Frederick J. Stare of Harvard University launched a coöperative study with Dr. W. J. E. Jessop of Trinity College, Dublin. So far some 500 pairs of brothers have been tracked down, where one brother has migrated to Boston while the

---

* "Saturated" means that the fat molecule contains all the hydrogen atoms it can hold. Unsaturated and polyunsaturated fats, mostly vegetable oils, have room in the molecule for additional hydrogen atoms.

other remained in Ireland. Striking facts turned up. The Boston brothers have a considerably higher heart-disease rate than those who remained behind—yet those in Ireland consume more animal fats and almost *twice* as much butter. The explanation? No one is sure. But one of the most significant differences between the two groups is that the Ireland brothers live active lives, doing heavy farm work, walking to work, etc. The Boston brothers drive cars, are mostly desk workers.

For over six years, Chicago's Dr. Oglesby Paul has followed the histories of 2000 middle-aged employees of a manufacturing concern. So far 130 cases of heart disease have appeared—divided almost exactly between those who ate high-fat diets, and those who ate low-fat diets. Navajo Indians provided another puzzler. In general they eat the same high-fat diet as other Americans, yet have only a fraction the heart disease.

The cholesterol riddle poses questions. Why does the blood's cholesterol level fluctuate so? Worry pushes it up, exercise drives it down. Thus, a man worrying about business might appear in grave danger, but a fortnight later, on vacation, he might appear in fine shape.

And if cholesterol is such an enemy, why don't we *all* get heart disease? One autopsy study of 300 people showed cholesterol deposits in the arteries of *all* over the age of seven. A study in Minneapolis showed that men aged 30 had 60 percent as much deposit material in their arteries as people who had died of heart disease.

If things have been puzzling in the clinic, they have been equally puzzling in the laboratory. At Columbia University's College of Physicians and Surgeons, Dr. Henry S. Simms examined human arteries removed at autopsy. Fatty deposits in artery walls, observed under the microscope, in the earliest stages of their accumulation *gave no indication of cholesterol at all!* They were mainly composed of triglycerides and other fatty materials. Cholesterol, apparently, didn't accumulate in observable quantities until later.

In a recent experiment, Harvard's Dr. David D. Rutstein made striking observations. He grew human artery cells in test tubes, nourishing them with blood serum. He would have prison volunteers eat a carefully composed meal—say, a high-fat meal—before drawing blood for his test-tube arteries. Some baffling observations followed. For example: *more* fat was deposited in the artery cells after meals rich in polyunsaturated fats than after saturated-fat meals! He also noted that fats were deposited in the artery cells when prisoners were fasting—indicating they were drawing on deposits of body fat.

As a result of work of this type, many physicians are today questioning the importance of cholesterol as a leading factor in the heart-disease problem. Although high blood levels of cholesterol are usually found in people with heart trouble, there is a growing suspicion that this may be not cause and effect, but purely associative. Says one researcher: "We could as well note that countries which have the most telephones and flush toilets also have the most heart disease."

Dr. Arthur M. Master, noted New York cardiologist, adds his voice: "Enthusiastic premature claims concerning the importance of polyunsaturated fatty acids in preventing coronary disease have been widespread. The ingestion of large amounts of these acids is unnecessary and may actually be harmful."

How then is the layman to resolve the question for himself?

Although the role of cholesterol may be in question, there is agreement that fats in general do play a role as a causative factor in heart disease. As things stand today, most physicians think that the 40 to 45 percent of our calories that come from fats should be cut to 25 to 30 percent. The American Heart Association concurs, urging a reduction of fats in diet—with a *reasonable* substitution of vegetable oils and other polyunsaturated fats for animal fats. A reduction of fats and of caloric intake would at least result in a loss of weight, and overweight is *known* to predispose to heart trouble.

In the *Journal of the American Medical Association,* Dr.

Master declares: "Many factors other than diet play a role in coronary disease, including emotion and behavior patterns, lack of physical exercise, excessive smoking, heredity and sex. Many non-fat nutrients appear to be involved: excess sodium, magnesium deficiency, extremes of protein and carbohydrate intake. In the present incomplete state of our knowledge, a drastic change in the diet is not justified."

Analysis

The title of this article indicates that it is a subject of high interest to many people: medical articles are normally well read, heart disease and strokes are our greatest killers, and cholesterol has been widely hailed as a culprit. Advertisers of various foods have emphasized low cholesterol content, and many people have changed their eating habits. The subject might seem to have been done to death, but the sub-title promises that "the defense now offers new evidence—in what may well be medicine's most important mystery."

The following outline shows how the article was developed:

The lead: a statement of the two sides of the controversy.

The theme: which follows, reinforces the lead by giving two authoritative but opposing medical opinions.

Transition to the body of the article: "The layman can only . . . examine the evidence."

Definition of cholesterol and its properties. The evidence against it: in Russia, Japan, Italy, Massachusetts. A summing up of the evidence against it. The reaction of people—many changed their diets.

Transition to opposing evidence: "Cautious research men weren't ready for such a leap."

Opposing evidence: brothers in Ireland and Boston; effects

of worry; the puzzle of the Navajo Indians, Minneapolis study, etc.

Transition to another thought: "If things have been puzzling in the clinic, they have been equally puzzling in the laboratory."

The laboratory findings.

Transition: "As a result of work of this type, many physicians are today questioning the importance of cholesterol as a leading factor in the heart-disease problem."

What the doctors say.

Transition to conclusion: "How then is the layman to resolve the question for himself?"

The conclusion: Role of cholesterol is in question; overweight is a factor; reduction of fats in the diet is recommended; list of other factors and other nutrients which appear to be involved. "In the present incomplete state of our knowledge, a drastic change in the diet is not justified." This final sentence brings the subject home to the reader.

Mr. Ratcliff's article is short—in the *Reader's Digest* tradition—but it is packed with information. A more leisurely piece would follow the same pattern: a high interest subject, a revealing title, a careful build-up of the argument with clear transitions from one section to another, and non-technical language.

If you are writing for a special magazine—say one on sailing—you can and usually should shift into the seaman's language. You can presuppose that your reader is acquainted with the sailing vocabulary and he would have no respect for your seamanship if you did not use it.

The same formula governs writing for any technical publication. You would not describe a monkey wrench for the readers of *Mechanix Illustrated* or explain the difference between a hare and a cottontail for the *Rabbit Growers' Gazette*. In any case, know the reader you are aiming at, and you will have greater chance of success.

The "think" piece

With the growing desire for education in the United States, there has also been a growing interest in what is called the "think" piece or the "egghead" article. These articles are usually found in magazines of comparatively small circulation, such as *The Atlantic, Harper's, The Reporter* and *The New Republic,* which are addressed to the more erudite members of our society. Occasionally you will find one in *Life, Esquire,* or *The Saturday Evening Post.* But not often.

We must distinguish between the informational article and the "think" piece by saying that the first tells *what* and the second *why.* But that isn't all. The "think" piece is not content merely to give information; it also analyzes the background of the subject and sets it against some large national or international issue. As an example, let us look at a hypothetical article.

You're writing of the newspaper strike in New York in 1962 and 1963 and the part played by Bertram A. Powers, president of the typographical local and by his union. Depending on your own point of view, you might portray Mr. Powers and his union members as mistreated people who were struggling only for their rights as Americans and for an adequate wage. Or you could show Mr. Powers as a black-hearted villain and the union as a power-obsessed group with no regard for their fellow citizens in New York. In either case, you might have an interesting and timely portrait.

You might move on to a discussion of the effect on New Yorkers, and on businesses such as department stores and theaters, of weeks and weeks without papers. In this you would have a good factual piece, but it would not be a "think" piece. However, you might go still further and indicate that this strike was merely the most recent incident in the long history of labor since the Industrial Revolution; or of strikes in the United States with emphasis on the printing trades. As you did your research, you would find that the first recorded strike by a union in our country was called by the Journeymen Printers in New York in 1776. That would set you to asking whether printers over the years had suffered special hardships.

You would look into the history of newspapers. Why are there each year fewer and fewer? What has been the influence of radio and television? Finally, you might consider how automation is dislocating labor especially in the printing trades. You might conclude with Telstar and the future of communications in the space age not only in America, but in the world.

You set Powers, the union and the strike in perspective against the backdrop of history and show this as a small part of a world problem. You would have a "think" piece.

This is the hardest kind of article to write; it takes research, leg work, endless digging and hours of planning. And it calls for a closer study by the reader than a more superficial article—that is the reason it is published in the more serious journals.

One of my students recently planned an article proving that within a few years automation may take over many of the jobs women have been doing—clerical and office and secretarial work, for instance. At the same time, more and more women are going to be needed in some of the professions, such as medicine, science, psychiatry, teaching and computer analysis. She planned to address her article to mothers, since professional work requires long periods of study and training and the girls should begin preparing in high school.

As she thought it over, more and more complications came to mind. In these days of early marriages and instant babies, how many girls would be willing to put off these delights for years of college, graduate school, and job training? How many girls want careers? Would mothers prefer to steer their daughters into matrimony? After all, what is woman's sphere? Is she bound by her biological functions?

She found herself wound up in the feminine mystique, masculine supremacy, social pressures and the population explosion. She realized that she could afford neither the time nor the effort to prepare an adequate article, and gave it up.

I cite this to show that the "think" piece is costly to produce.

Add to that the knowledge that the magazines which publish these articles usually cannot afford to pay as well as the large-circulation journals.

Why then should a writer attempt a "think" piece? Sometimes the subject is one to which he is almost religiously committed, and he must get it out of his system. (If you do not feel strongly about your subject, better drop it in any case.) Even established writers can afford such an article only once in a while. But the reward in satisfaction is great.

The other reward is prestige. Most editors scan their

immediate competition carefully and glance through a score of other journals. But the publications they take home to read for ideas are likely to be the "egghead" magazines such as *The Reporter, Commentary, Harper's, The Atlantic.* If an editor likes an article in one of these, he will note the author's name as a good prospect for his own journal. A writer I know, who had confined her writing to technical economic journals, wrote a piece on a less technical subject which was accepted by *Harper's.* Within two weeks of its appearance, she had letters from the editors of three other publications asking her to come to lunch to discuss ideas.

Should a writer specialize?

This is a question that every beginning writer asks sooner or later. My answer is that my own small specialty helped me get started; at least it got me editorial jobs.

The subject I started with, come upon by happenstance, was children. I had had summer jobs at an excellent girls' camp in Vermont. I helped with horseback riding, typed long letters from the director to parents telling of the progress of their children, and edited a camp paper. After the first summer, the director asked me to write a short piece about our experience in comforting lonely or homesick girls. The piece was printed under my name in a camp director's annual—my first by-line. At the same camp, I met the editor of *The American Girl,* the Girl Scout magazine, and persuaded her to let me write short pieces for girls on behavior, grooming, etc. At the end of two years, my small scrapbook of pieces for or about children got me an editorial job with a weekly for high school students. A year and a half later, I went to *The American*

Girl and later became its editor. When I was ready to tackle the adult field, my experience made the transition possible.

When I speak of a specialty, I am thinking of subjects such as medicine, child health, child guidance, education, travel, finance, architecture, city planning, home skills, automobiles, natural history, hobbies, science, art, music, hi-fi—the list is endless. Some subjects offer more outlets for your writing than others—more publications want articles on health than on *petit point* embroidery. However, research in one subject may lead you to others. The embroidery might suggest all forms of handwork, and on to interior decoration. From child guidance you might move into education, adolescent problems, etc.

The genesis of some specialities may be a special interest you found at college; or you may have acquired an interest through experience and your own reading. Or you may have taken some special courses after college. Some schools of journalism, for instance, offer special courses in science writing.

The advantages of a specialty are many. When an editor has accepted you as a careful and accurate and dependable reporter for your special subject, he will think of you when he is looking for a writer in your field and will listen with respect when you suggest articles from the bailiwick you have staked out for yourself.

Also—and not to be disdained—as you accumulate a list of publications that take your work, you have a dependable source of checks. The checks may be small at first but can grow with your own proficiency.

Another plus is that you can often work up your specialty, almost as a hobby, while you are earning a living at something else or bringing up a family. I know four writers, otherwise employed, who write regularly for religious home magazines; a furniture dealer who contributes human interest pieces to the home furnishings trade press; two mothers who, having started with first-person articles about their children, have now acquired professional collaborators and write on child health and guidance for large national magazines; school teachers who are writing textbooks; a fisherman with a ready market for his catch of advice and adventures; newspapermen who have profitable sidelines as political and financial writers for business journals.

Still another advantage: while you are researching one article, you often run across salable ideas for others. The reading you do for each article increases your own store of knowledge, and as you interview one person after another in your field, you will come to have at your fingertips a list of authorities to whom you can go time and again for information.

You need not become a doctor to write about medicine —few doctors can write at all. That is not surprising. While you were learning to become a writer, the doctor was studying medicine. As writers you and he are collaborators: he supplies the facts, and you translate them into words that are interesting and intelligible to the reader. However, you must know enough about your field to ask intelligent questions and to make a lucid report of what he tells you.

On the other hand, if you are writing "how to" articles, you had better know "how to." I have never known a convincing writer on food who did not love to eat and know how to cook; nor a good writer on gardens who did not himself grow vegetables and flowers in his own back yard. But, a successful food writer will also be up on the principles of nutrition and new items appearing on the supermarket shelves; and the garden writer will have come to know the leading nurserymen and the new varieties of zinnias and cabbages that are being developed.

Much of the above advice is superfluous. If you are really stirred up about a subject, your own curiosity will prod you to ferret out every possible fact and facet of the subject. There are some qualifications you should cultivate:

You should become a skillful interviewer. You will be picking the brains of authorities in your field, and it is imperative that you establish a friendly relationship with them. Often professional men take tactful handling.

You must be a good reporter, and that means getting down the facts or opinions accurately. You will certainly check your statements with your authority to make sure, but if you have misunderstood or misquoted him, he may lack confidence in you for the future. Accuracy will also win you the respect of your editor.

And finally, you should read the professional journals or trade press and new books that pertain to your subject in order to keep up with the latest developments—a new angle can bring to life a well-worn subject. As you saw earlier, J. D. Ratcliff, one of our leading medical writers, used a new finding effectively in his article on cholesterol.

ℵ 15

WRITING AND REWRITING

You HAVE RUN a fresh sheet of paper into your typewriter; your notebook items are numbered or your folders of notes are neatly arranged. The moment of decision has come, and you've nothing to do but to write. And paralysis sets in.

First one sentence then another rolls through your mind. None seems right. You look at your notes, find a quote or anecdote, but decide to save it for later in the piece. You get up and look out the window. You think of a dozen chores you ought to do, and suddenly they seem very important and attractive. You remind yourself that this is the time to write and resolutely go back to the typewriter.

The one way to start is—*to start*.

Try one of these ways to break your log jam. Imagine you are writing to an old friend who would be interested in your subject. Write informally and easily and tell him all about it. Or imagine that several years have gone by and you are recalling this article. What will stick in your mind then? Begin with that.

Either of these should get you started down the road to your destination. Keep that destination in mind, but otherwise just keep going. Don't worry about your lead or whether this paragraph should go before or after that one. If you have forgotten an item, don't try to find the right place to put it, just start a new paragraph with it. Don't worry about sentence structure, syntax or length. Consult your free-wheeling outline occasionally, if you like, but don't go back for verification to your notes. All that can come in a later draft. Go right on to the end.

Willy-nilly, you will have your first draft.

Practical note: It's a good idea to triple-space this first draft, so there will be room for corrections and revisions.

It is probably too long and, in your final revision, you may not use any of it just as you have put it down. But you've got something concrete in front of you that you can see and handle instead of a lot of vague suggestions that go round and round in your mind. If you have time, take a day or half day off so you can return to it fresh.

Revision

Then start to revise. First study the organization. Is the order as you have written it effective? Would you have a faster start if you put more case histories nearer the beginning? Have you worked toward a strong closing, or would a rearrangement help that also? If any of these apply, and probably all will, cut your text apart, rearrange and make a new outline, which can now be more detailed. Check your copy with your notes to make sure you have not omitted some important point. Also check your facts, your anecdotes and quotes for accuracy.

Don't throw away your first draft, or any subsequent one, until after your piece has been accepted. While you'll probably use very little of it, you may later recall that you had an especially telling sentence or phrase and want to look at it again.

Now tackle your second draft. Don't copy whole chunks from your first draft. You are writing more carefully now, so rework your paragraphs to fit your new conception. If on reading your second draft, you feel that your organization is good, then start to edit.

How is the length? It is probably still too long, so look for cuts. Take out anything that is irrelevant, that does not move the article along. Sharpen your use of words. Cut out jargon, take a look at the grammar, check facts again. If in the middle of the night you suddenly have the nagging feeling that something you wrote may not be accurate, or a passage in the manuscript now seems coy or affected, check in the morning and make the necessary changes. And be sure you haven't written over your readers' heads. Keep in mind that your purpose is not to impress your readers with your own erudition but to leave a thought or fact or an emotion with them. Don't forget Raymond Clapper's well-known admonition, "Never underestimate the intelligence or overestimate the information of the public."

Look at your paragraphs. Keep them short. Long paragraphs make for hard reading and invite the reader to skip. The same goes for sentences. Here let your ear guide you. Short sentences, one after another, give a staccato effect and suggest action. Overlong sentences make a reader nod. A combination of long and short makes for an easier style. By long I mean not more than thirty or forty words.

By this time you should be ready for your third draft. Perhaps the perfect lead has already come to you. If not, write your third draft, then tackle the lead and conclusion, so that, hopefully, your fourth draft will be complete. But don't be downhearted if you have to make still another go at it.

Before you go into your final draft, check every paragraph to make sure it says what you mean. You may find you have written in generalities when you need specifics. If so, or if you find a fuzzy paragraph, ask yourself, "Just what did I mean here?" Then rewrite that paragraph in simple, ABC words. It will probably be more effective than your original version.

To illustrate what revising and rewriting will do for an article, here is the first draft of a short piece written by Joseph Vecchione for a company house organ, which published short pieces concerning their employees. (The names have been changed.)

Stock Car Safety Inspector
Bob Bligh's Weekend Role

For Bob Bligh life is just one race after another. At least on weekends that is. That's when Wilson Company's foreman Bligh changes roles and becomes a National Association for Stock Car Auto Racing (NASCAR) Safety Inspector.

If you're one of the more than 8000 fans who visit the Ellington Speedway on the Ellington Fair Grounds on Saturday nights during the racing season, Bob is the guy you've seen taking a close look at stock cars which have come to a sudden stop—the hard way. One of his many duties is to see to it that any vehicle which is involved in a collision gets a safety once-over before resuming a race.

His real heavy work, though, takes place long before the race starts. That's when he checks closely the fifty or sixty cars which will race on a given night, and sees to it that all NASCAR safety requirements are met.

"I can hear the boys in the pits saying 'here he comes' when I start my rounds," Bob says. "And there's many a thing I must look for. Safety belts must be of a special width, seats have to be welded or bolted to the car frame, doors must be welded shut, gas tanks are required to be mounted in trunks and secured in such a manner they will not shift if a car flips, fuel lines must run under the car body and not through the car, exhaust pipes must be angled so fumes don't enter the car and any number of other important regulations must be strictly adhered to. These regulations are designed to protect the driver in any situation he might meet out on the track.

"Some of the boys can use colorful language when I have to reject their cars from a race, but I have the last say. If anything's wrong they don't race. Neither I or NASCAR will have it any other way."

For a man who became interested in stock car racing by watching a friend whiz around a track some twenty years ago, Bob isn't much of a spectator today. "I'm a physical wreck when a race is on," he says. "I know all of the boys out there and it's like watching your own family coming down the home stretch at 90 miles an hour. As the safety man I feel responsible for them. I spend the whole race hoping nothing will happen."

His hopes, however, have been dashed many a time. But they've been answered in another way. He's seen all kinds of collisions, even a triple flip-over once, but nobody has ever been killed or seriously injured.

The emphasis on safety doesn't end with the last race of the night either. Bob carries it over into his personal life.

For a guy who spends Saturday nights listening to the squeal of breaks, it's understandable.

The faults of this are obvious: The lead is slow and unless you knew Bligh or were interested in stock car racing, you would probably never read past it. In the fourth sentence, the town is identified twice within six words.

The dialogue isn't convincing—Bligh would probably never have used a sentence as long as the one beginning with "safety belts." The ending is weak—we are told that Bligh carries his concern for safety over to his personal life, but not how he does so.

Yet there was material here for an action-filled short portrait. After two revisions, this is what the writer came up with:

FOR BOB BLIGH
LIFE IS ONE RACE AFTER ANOTHER

The nerve jangling squeal of red hot car brakes desperately gripping the wheels is a familiar sound to Wilson foreman Bob Bligh. He hears it often on Saturday nights as safety inspector for the National Association for Stock Car Auto Racing (NASCAR) at the Ellington Speedway.

"The sounds of brakes I can take," he says, "but the noise of a crash sends a chill down my spine. There are those eternal seconds when no one knows just how bad the crash is. The first thing I think of is—will the driver get out all right? And the next—did he crash because I missed something during the safety examination before the race?

"If the crowd roars, I know the driver has waved that he's O.K. Then I look at the car. That lets me decide if the car can continue to race."

It's obvious even on short acquaintance that the responsibility for the safety of the drivers weighs heavily on Bob. Because "he checks everything as closely as a father would before allowing his son to get behind the wheel of a racer," the drivers call him "the old man". But sandy-haired Bob, whose solid 42-year-old frame stretches to a towering six feet two inches, looks anything but an old man as he makes his inspection rounds before the races.

Every car *must* meet strict safety requirements. Each car *must* have safety belts of a certain width. Seats *must* be welded or bolted to the car frame. Doors *must* be welded shut. Gas tanks *must* be mounted in trunks and attached firmly so they don't shift if a car flips. Fuel lines *must* run under the car body and not through the car. Exhaust pipes *must* be angled so fumes don't enter the car. These are a few of the many regulations.

To the drivers in a fifty-car waiting line the list seems endless, but they wait patiently. As Bob explains, "They know the regulations are to protect them in any situation on the track. That isn't to say that some of the boys don't use colorful language if I bar a car from racing. But I close my ears and keep my eyes open. I have the last say. If anything's wrong they don't race. I won't have it any other way, and NASCAR won't either."

For a man who became interested in stock car racing by watching a friend whiz around a track some twenty years ago, Bob isn't much of a spectator today. "I'm a physical wreck when a race is on. I know all the boys out there and it's like watching my own family coming down the home stretch at 90 miles an hour. I spend the whole race hoping nothing will happen."

His hopes, however, have been dashed many a time. But they've been answered in another way. He's seen all kinds of collisions, even a triple flip-over once, but nobody has ever been killed or seriously injured.

Bob's emphasis on safety doesn't end with the last race of the night. He carries it over to his personal life. The last sound he hears before starting his own car engine for the trip home is the click of his safety belt.

The improvement in this rewrite is equally obvious. Since this is an action piece, the writer starts with an action lead, then identifies his subject and places the scene in one sentence. He builds his theme in the next three paragraphs of quotes which sound authentic; then proceeds to the down-to-earth aspects of Bligh's insistence on safe cars for the race.

The safety specifications for the racing cars are now given in the third person and are broken up into short sentences. The repetition of "must" gives emphasis. Next follow his relations with the drivers, his own emotions, and the results of his safety precautions. The closing tells how his insistence on safety carries over to his own driving.

Many young writers are surprised to learn that even professionals rewrite over and over in order to pinpoint the effect they wish, and are equally surprised at the revisions they also must make. Often they are so enchanted with the idea that they have completed an article that they are blind to its faults.

I find this easy to understand. Once for a short period

I enrolled in a class in oil painting and produced two small still lifes, one of a bowl of eggs and one of a vase of chrysanthemums. I was forced to give up the class but occasionally I come across my maiden efforts in an old portfolio and even today I look at them with admiration. "Isn't it wonderful that I painted them," I tell myself. I realize in my more sober moments that they are just beginner's exercises, that one of the eggs looks like a bald head, and that I would have had to work for a long time to produce even a barely professional painting. But I can still recapture the excitement of my own creation.

Fortunately my own early writing was done under the critical eye of a fine editor who handed my short items back time and again, or, even more damaging to my pride, finally rewrote them himself, showing me clearly where I was wrong.

If you are working without a professional eye over your shoulder, then look at your own work critically. Margery Allingham is quoted by Paul Reynolds in his book *The Writing and Selling of Non-Fiction* (Doubleday) as stating:

> I write every paragraph four times—once to get my meaning down, once to put in anything I have left out, once to take out anything that seems unnecessary, and once to make the whole thing sound as if I had only just thought of it.

Here are some of my own struggles with the recalcitrant first paragraph of a 400-word review of *The Glamour Magazine Party Book* by Eleanor Thomas Elliott. The book is addressed to the hostess in today's usually servantless household. As I read, I had made notes of

what I would say in the body of the review, and when I
came to cast about for a lead, I remembered having once
seen a statement in Mrs. Emily Post's book, *Etiquette,*
warning hostesses against ever hiring a man servant with
a mustache. I thought this might make an amusing opening, so I whipped over to the library to look at the various
editions of Mrs. Post's book. I found that she had carried
the warning to her last edition, published only ten years
ago. A few sentences contrasting her time with today and
her book with Mrs. Elliott's would seem simple enough,
but here are some of my tries at the first sentence:

First: "Casual living has moved at better than a snail's
pace since, a mere ten years ago, Mrs. Emily Post felt constrained to advise the hostess that 'it should be unnecessary
to add that none but the unwitting would employ a butler
or any other house servant who wears a mustache.'" Since
the subject of Mrs. Elliott's book was our social life, that
should be included. Mrs. Post's "it should be unnecessary
to add" added nothing, so—

Second: "Casual living has moved into our social life at
better than a snail's pace since, a mere ten years ago, Mrs.
Emily Post felt constrained to advise the hostess that 'none
but the unwitting would employ a butler or any other
house servant who wears a mustache.'" I felt I should
make the point that men servants were vanishing; "justified" seemed a better word than "constrained," so—

Third: "Casual living has moved into our lives as men
servants have moved out at better than a snail's pace,
since a mere ten years ago, Mrs. Emily Post felt justified
in advising, etc."

Fourth: I realized that I had fallen in love with the
cliché "at a snail's pace," and bade it farewell in my fourth

try. But I felt Mrs. Post's power as a social arbiter should be mentioned—the younger women might not realize it. So I took a new start.

Fifth: "It was a mere ten years ago when men servants were so available that Mrs. Emily Post in her stalwart volume which has guided generations of American women, still felt it necessary to warn that, etc." Whoops! Too long for an opening. So, the final version:

"It is only ten years since the appearance of the last edition of Mrs. Emily Post's stalwart volume which has guided generations of American women through the social ritual. Even at that late date, men servants were still so available that she felt it advisable to warn hostesses that 'none but the unwitting would employ a butler or any other house servant who wears a mustache.' "

That hurdle passed, I could go on to my next paragraph: "Today's party giver often numbers as her staff only an obliging husband (sometimes mustached or even bearded), or, if she is unmarried, a guest host to make the cocktails, carve the roast and pour the wine."

From that point, it was easy enough to fit in the body of the piece and end by saying the book was helpful both to the experienced and inexperienced hostess. The last sentence gave me a little trouble.

My first rather pompous try read, "The inexperienced hostess may well be led through her first party giving to that precious (perfect? prized?) moment when, the last guest having been ushered out, the young host turns to his bride and bestows the prized accolade, 'It was a good party. You did yourself proud.' " Phew!

I cleaned that up to, "The inexperienced hostess may be led through her first company dinner to the moment when, the last guest having left, the young husband locks the door and bestows the prized accolade, 'It *was* a nice party!' "

It should be easy to express one's meaning in simple declarative sentences and homely, unpretentious words. But often it is not.

Carry-over

One other hint to keep your writing going: When the time comes to stop for the day and you have also reached the end of a portion of your piece, don't stop with the sentence that ends that thought. Stay on and, while your brain is still in high gear, write the first sentence or two of the next point you will make. Having this much start will save you the time you would otherwise spend the next day getting yourself back into the mood of your article.

ℵ 16

THE USE AND MAGIC OF WORDS

THE PRIMARY USE of words is simply and forthrightly to say what we mean. The small child with his limited vocabulary does exactly this. "I don't like it," he says, and pushes his cereal bowl off his high chair or the table. "I want that," he announces, and yanks a toy from his playmate.

It is only when we have acquired a much larger vocabulary, and when what we wish to express is more complicated and more subtle, or we think it is, that we often let our use of words obscure thought rather than express it.

There are several reasons for this state of affairs.

The first lies at the door of our boasted system of American education, which rarely teaches a student to write. Occasionally a lucky student in high school or even in college, has a teacher who loves literature and language and words and is able to pass his own enthusiasm on to his pupils.

The art and the craft

Even if you are one of those who face the future with a meager knowledge of how to put one word after another to make sense, all is not lost. It is true that writing is an art and some are born with it; but it is also a craft and one that you can teach yourself.

Sometimes you fail to say what you mean because you're not sure what you *do* mean. In one of Marya Mannes' little essays in *Book Week* (December 8, 1963), she tells of an English teacher who asked one of her pupils what she though Keats meant by the "still unravished bride of quietness." The young lady's answer was that she knew what Keats meant but couldn't express it. To which the teacher snapped, "If you know it, you can express it." Among the maxims I advise you to paste over your typewriter, include that one.

I am also reminded of a very talkative lady whose out-of-patience husband asked one day, "Why do you talk so much?" Her answer was, "How am I going to know what I think if I don't say it?" The same idea is expressed by Janet Teissier Du Cros in her book, *Divided Loyalties*. An Englishwoman living in France, she writes, "Like Pericles the French consider that until thought has found verbal expression it is scarcely worthy of the name of thought."

To apply that maxim to your writing, discover what you really mean by putting it down on paper. You may find that you don't know. In that case, think it through until your mind is clear; then revise your sentence or paragraph. Often in the fervor of composition you discover that you are lacking a fact, and you let the words dance around in hope of covering up the deficiency. A simple solution is to stop writing and find the fact.

Sometimes the writer has immersed himself in his subject so thoroughly that when he comes to set it down he forgets the reader, and leaves out the information that would keep the reader with him. To avoid this, when you come to the final revision of your manuscript, before every paragraph ask yourself, "Will the reader understand this?" If the answer is "no," then rewrite the paragraph and insert the missing links.

Obscure sentences or paragraphs of any kind are the bane of an editor's life. When Harold Ross, late editor of *The New Yorker*, came across anything unclear, he would write "what mean" in the margin and ship the article back to the writer. Another editor calls the writer on the telephone, reads him the meaningless passage, and asks, "Just what are you trying to say here?" The writer explains in simple language, which the editor takes down, rewrites the paragraph in the writer's clear version, and thereby improves the manuscript.

A writer who is guilty too often of this sort of hidden meaning can exhaust the patience of his editor and so lose a market. Better clear it up yourself before submitting the article.

Clarity and color

In his *New York Times* review of *The Proud Tower* by Barbara Tuchman, Martin Duberman says, "The ability to write well (which must in any case be defined according to particular purpose) is more likely to be a symptom of clear thinking than a substitute for it."

The word that sums all this up is "precise." A book on

anthropology which I read some time ago with delight was *A Million Years of Man* by Richard Carrington, an English writer and scholar. After a longish description of some historical event he would say, "Now to precise the point," and sum up his argument with a sentence or two, so clearly and explicitly stated that even a tyro could not miss his meaning. His expression is one I return to again and again in my classes in writing. So often that last Christmas I had a note from an ex-student in which she said, "You dinned 'precise the point' into us until now I can't forget it even when I speak to my cat."

On the other hand, an article whose meaning is perfectly clear may become a dull and prosy piece. Your choice of words may resuscitate it. For this purpose, think of words as color. Once an artist has blocked in the structure of his composition, he turns to his palette of colors to bring vitality, mood, and emotion to his picture. So the writer can use words to bring action (vitality), mood, and emotion to his writing.

Along this line I think of Caroline Duer, whom I came to know and admire during the short time in my youth when I worked on *Vogue*. Miss Duer was the authority on manners, etiquette and *noblesse oblige* for *Vogue* and dictated answers to readers who wrote in to ask questions on behavior. She also wrote a little essay for every issue on whatever subject interested her—and her interests were wide. She had a taste for what she called mouth-filling words, and I recall with special pleasure an essay she wrote on the subject of words in the issue of *Vogue* for February 1, 1953, a few years before her death at ninety-plus:

A *blunderbus* seems to me much more explosive than a pistol, and *Beelzebub* twice as alarming as the Devil. *Rascal* and *rapscallion,* words constantly used by my two grandfathers over their Madeira, and generally when referring to old acquaintances, were well and favorably known to me from early childhood. *Scalawag* belonged in this group, as did *nincompoop, numbskull,* and *curmudgeon. Rambunctious* and *cantankerous* rumbled in the nursery. . . . To *bamboozle* must be more fun than to cheat and less likely to land one in prison. *Buxom* conveys a charm which *fat* entirely lacks; and *beholden* a kind of high graciousness in accepting favors which is missing in thankfulness. . . . *Lackadaisical* has a delightful sound, conveying much more than affectedly languid, and *dastardly* is a mouth-filling word—if ever there was one—unhappily to be used about a great many controversies in the world today. *Pandemonium* would describe most of our quite unnecessary squabbles, of which the Powers Above must be heartily tired.

I should like to think that our gifted young writers would bring to their choice of words the same gusto and meticulous selection.

This quotation is reprinted in Charles Ferguson's book, *Say It With Words,* and in my classes when we come to this subject, we read his book and take up a session or two playing some of the word games he suggests as exercises to stretch the vocabulary. One assignment is to start with A and go through the alphabet composing alliterative phrases and sentences. Some of my students' efforts were apt and amusing:

"The nasty necessity for never"

"Giddy as God on the day of creation"
"Baleful Beelzebub belching forth brimstone"
"Presumptuous pedants parading parody"
"Zany zealots espousing Zen"

We tried internal alliteration, too, as "Gone is the gondola from the Grand Canal," where there is a repetition of g's at the beginning and n's within the words. We composed metaphors and rhymes inspired by Ogden Nash.

While I would not suggest that such studied alliteration appear in your prose, I do recommend the practice as a word game to shake you free from clichés and trite expressions that disfigure so much prose. To quote Mr. Ferguson, these figures of speech "keep us on the line of discovery," so that "the mind is not caged by words or held back by the drags of conventional usage."

Playing with rhymes and rhythms, trying your hand at poetry and certainly reading it, brings another element to your writing—that of tone and cadence. Edna St. Vincent Millay, protesting indignantly to a procrastinating printer, wrote: "Do not for one moment . . . fan yourself with the cooling thought that I fail to see what is going on here and how gradually you have managed to sneak two weeks extra, then three weeks extra. . . ." She could, of course, have written: "Don't fool yourself that I don't see how you have put off and put off. . . ." But trained as a poet, she could not write even a business note without bringing to it such an effective phrase as "fan yourself with the cooling thought." Nor would a less precise writer than Wolcott Gibbs have said that the costumes in a Victorian play make the women "as beautiful and as sexless as yachts."

Using words effectively

Now to "precise the point," let us look at the effective use of individual words:

Nouns. Keep them explicit. Instead of "food" how about, "ham and eggs," "turnip greens with corn pone," "baked haddock;" "strawberries with cream," or "lollipops or peanut brittle or fudge" instead of "sweets." And shun such overworked generalities as "factors": "Many factors contributed to the President's decision on Viet Nam." All right, what were they? If you don't know, find out.

Definitive nouns are more descriptive than fuzzy adjectives. And, similarly, keep your antecedents straight; be sure the pronoun refers to the right noun. "She pushed the pram down the street; it was bumpy and full of holes." What was bumpy and full of holes, the pram or the street? Instead write, "She pushed the pram down the bumpy and pock-marked street."

Adjectives modify nouns and the rule again is to make them descriptive. If you say merely that the girl had a pretty face, you might as well forget it. But, "her smooth, dark hair framed the perfect oval of her face," makes a picture.

Adverbs modify verbs and, like adjectives, should work. And trite adverbs should be replaced by strong verbs: "She walked slowly toward the dean's office" is less effective than "She dragged her feet as she neared the dean's office." *Slowly, angrily, hesitantly, gladly, thankfully* used over and over become tiresome and meaningless.

In any case, blue-pencil both adjectives and adverbs unless they really do a job. For examples of good descriptive prose with a minimum of both adjectives and adverbs, read Hemingway.

Verbs are the pivot around which your sentence revolves. They can give action, movement, and emotion, so choose them with care. Say, he *walked,* and you have said little. But say he *ran, loped, staggered, swerved, took both sides of the street, sneaked by, lumbered, lurched, shambled,* and you give the reader a mental image. Instead of he *expressed his displeasure,* look at the effect of he *glared, raged, growled, snapped, ranted, frowned, fretted.*

The active voice is more effective than the passive. For instance, "His car knocked down six pedestrians" is better than, "Six pedestrians were knocked down by his car": and "She trusted him" is preferred to "He was trusted by her."

And finally some general rules:

Jargon

1. Cut out jargon such as, "It is a fact that." Not: "It is a fact that traffic is worse in Paris than in New York;" "Traffic is worse in Paris than in New York" is sufficient. And instead of, "In the case of underprivileged children school breakfasts are provided." Why not, "Breakfasts are provided at school for underprivileged children"?

2. Use overworked "in" words sparingly. Among the current favorites is *viable.* We read that the state of Jordan is "viable"; so is the Republican party. It simply means that both will probably survive. And *dedicated.* We have "dedicated" pigeon feeders, and "dedicated" Peace Corps members. Also overused are *escalation, expertise, dialogue,* and *mystique.* I am sick of *trauma* for an un-

happy childhood experience and of *alienated* young men who can't find themselves.

It seems to me that our social scientists are responsible for much jargon. I recently heard two of these eminent professionals arguing. At the conclusion one said, "In spite of the dichotomy we can aspire to an eventual symbiosis." Piffle! Why not, "In spite of our differences, I hope we'll eventually get together to our mutual profit"?

All of these are meaningful words and many of them say in a word what would otherwise take several words to express. But many writers use them indiscriminately to exhibit their own erudition. My advice is, don't write over your readers' heads and don't try to show off.

3. Don't underestimate your readers' intelligence and write down to him. But do keep your language easy and conversational.

There has been a great brouhaha among grammarians and purists these recent years over the growing habit among Americans of turning nouns and adjectives into verbs, and verbs into nouns and otherwise scrambling English diction. The English frown on it, and I find myself first on one side of the fence and then on the other. The use of the noun *contact* as a verb raises my hackles, partly because it is imprecise. Why not say to *speak* or *write* to or *telephone* or *wire* or *cable* or whatever the means of contact is. And yet *telephoned, wired* and *cabled* are all nouns turned into verbs. Also "contacted" seems to me a harsh, ugly word that grates on my ears. I am sure, too, that I could never be comfortable in the company of a person who said "he finalized the deal." And yet I found myself *pleasured* at the aptness of Leo Rosten's "The thought *miserabled* me," in a recent copy of *Look*.

Finally "to precise this point," I would not undertake to give any writer absolute rules on this subject. Here it is each to his own taste. The same is true of turning verbs into nouns whether you take your car in for a "check-up" or yourself to the doctor for the same purpose.

ℵ 17

STYLE

THERE ARE PROBABLY as many definitions of style as there are ways of cooking hamburger. They range from Swift's "proper words in proper places", to Buffon's "a man's style is part of him." *The American College Dictionary* defines it as "characteristic mode of writing or speaking, as determined by period, literary form, personality, etc." Chesterton says it is "the dress of thought," and Pater holds that it is "a certain absolute and unique manner of expressing a thing, in all its intensity and color." Charles Ferguson interprets it as "our personal appearance in print, our self-image given speech."

Foundations

Let us begin by looking at the foundations on which a writer builds his own style: *clarity, communication, conviction,* and *contagious enthusiasm.*

Clarity has been discussed elsewhere, as the writer's ability to know what he means, to say it, and finally to communicate his meaning to the reader. The two characters in this "dialogue" are the writer and the reader, and unless the communication between the two is clear, the reader will feel cheated no matter how eloquently the writer may express his own personality.

Think of yourself as a cook who has prepared a delicious meal. If you keep it out of the reach of the diner, he will go away hungry and the culinary skill you have put into the preparation of your offering will be wasted.

The second building stone of your foundation is *conviction*—call it commitment, if you like, or conscience. If you are to write convincingly, you must believe in what you are saying. You should approach your subject seriously and honestly. If you don't believe that the idea you are presenting is important, you won't make a contribution to your reader's thought or action, and you should give up the article. If you hate modern architecture, don't try to write a laudatory piece on Frank Lloyd Wright.

However, you may change the emphasis of your article. One of my students once attempted to write an article for a trade magazine on saunas—the Finnish hot baths which were becoming popular. He had heard glowing reports on them, and his research and interviews bolstered this point of view. Then he visited such a bath and tried it out himself. He emerged with the conviction that this was an invention of the devil and that only a Scandinavian would subject himself to such punishment. He turned his presentation around and wrote an amusing piece, laughing at them in a good-humored way. Needless to say, he lost his first market, but others were open.

On the other hand, you may be assigned a subject

about which you don't, at the outset, feel strongly. But as you get into your research, read, talk with the authorities, and study the subject from different angles, you may find that your interest grows, and by the time you sit down at your typewriter, you have become a convert and can't wait to tell the world about your discovery.

Contagious enthusiasm is your third building block. If you have it you will convey it to the reader, and your piece will have vitality. Any editor can spot enthusiasm on the first page of a manuscript. Lack of it produces a dull piece and leads to many a rejection slip. Good writing is emotional writing. I don't mean overblown emoting; but enthusiasm is not communicated by the use of such ubiquitous adverbs as *beautifully, wonderfully, excitingly,* etc. Instead, express your eagerness through descriptive nouns and action verbs.

With clarity, conviction and enthusiasm in your writing, you are on the way to becoming a good writer.

A style that fits

Many writers when they are hopefully aiming an article at a particular magazine, undertake to write in what they consider the style of that publication. This, more often than not, is a useless maneuver. At *McCall's* I once turned down a manuscript in which we had expressed an interest only to have the author say, "But I wrote it in the *McCall's* style." My answer was, "The style of whatever contributor you were copying is suitable neither to your subject nor to the point of view you are trying to put across."

Most general magazines today like a variety of subjects

in each issue, and each piece is written in a style that fits
its subject. We used to hear about *The Saturday Evening
Post's* style. But a recent issue has the following articles:

>*Only Fools Laugh at Their Woes,* by Angus Wilson
>(A gently written piece that tells about different kinds
>of humor and when humor does not fill the bill).
>
>*"Each Man Kills the Thing He Loves,"* by Stewart
>Alsop (An essay on fox hunting).
>
>Also by Mr. Alsop, *Robert McNamara: His Business
>Is War* (A serious profile of the Secretary of Defense
>defining his stand on international affairs, and the pres-
>sures he labors under).
>
>*The Short-Order Cocktail,* by Ogden Nash (A typical
>Nash poem on the servantless household).
>
>*Lauren Bacall: She Travels by Roller Coaster,* by
>Thomas Meehan (A sympathetic profile of Miss Bacall).
>
>*Drugs on the Campus,* by Richard Goldstein (A se-
>rious but readable discussion of that current dilemma).
>
>*Jose Torres: The Lost Hero,* by Pete Hamill (A sym-
>pathetic, but human portrait of a fighter).
>
>*Panic in Chicago's Mafia,* by Bill Davidson and Sandy
>Smith (Again a serious piece on the FBI's war on gang-
>sters).

If you were aiming at the *Post,* whose footsteps would
you try to follow? Alsop the essayist or Alsop the com-
mentator? Ogden Nash or Pete Hamill? Leaf through
any publication on your reading table and you will find
much the same variety.

Even in magazines with a definite editorial bent such
as *Esquire,* each piece has its individual style. The *subject matter* and the *writer's point of view* determine the

way in which the piece is written and the magazine for which it is suitable.

You should give careful consideration, however, to possible markets for your articles. For instance, you know that politically some magazines lean to the left, others to the right; that *Look* is fast-paced, and *Harper's* generally serious; that the *Reader's Digest* likes the upbeat, and *The Nation* views with alarm. So by all means read several issues of the magazine to which you plan to submit your articles. (I have had young applicants for a job come into *McCall's* without having given the magazine more than a cursory glance.) You would certainly not submit the same article to *Playboy* and to *The Atlantic*.

When you study a magazine thoroughly, you will come to understand its audience. The editor knows his readers (if he didn't he wouldn't hold his job), and it is with their interests in mind that he makes his selections and establishes the pattern into which his editorial material usually falls. But observe, too, that every magazine often breaks its own pattern. One well-known editor insisted that every issue should have at least one surprise in it. You can't make hard and fast rules. Also take into consideration that you will want more than one market. An article on child behavior, for instance, might be turned down by the *Ladies' Home Journal,* and if the style is right for its subject, it may find a place in *McCall's,* one of the Sunday magazines, *Good Housekeeping, Parents', Redbook,* or an educational journal.

A style of your own

Just as any novice writer looks forward to the day when he achieves a by-line, so he wants to give his work the personal imprint that marks it uniquely his own. Every child, as soon as he speaks or learns to write, has his own style. Little Susie does not use words in the same way as does little George and as they grow they carry their personal ways of expression into adulthood.

Think of the letters you receive from your friends and family. Even without the handwriting and postmark, you know instinctively that a certain letter is from Aunt Mary; you would never confuse it even on a post card with that of another Mary who may live in the same town and have the same interests.

But when you begin to use language to convey ideas, information and emotion, you become eager to develop a style that is an expression of yourself. This is not mere vanity or egotism. Your reading tells you that each good writer has a manner of personal expression. So do musicians. You recognize the difference between Bach and Beethoven, and you would not confuse Wagner with Webern. In painting you recognize that Raphael's style is different from that of Goya.

But though each of us has a style, we are not endowed at birth with a good style; that is acquired. Many writers reach their own personal expression by deliberately trying to write like some admired author. This is not bad, if you know when to stop.

Somerset Maugham in *The Summing Up* tells how in his youth he tried successively to ape the styles of Pater, Wilde, Swift and Dryden, until, after five years, he realized that he was writing contrary to his own bent. He had learned something from each, but it was not until he took stock of his own capacities—an acute power of observation, a logical sense and an appreciation of the sound of words—that he came into his own. His lucidity, simplicity and euphony made him an outstanding success of his time. I would not advise that you copy Maugham for style but you can learn much from him as a master of logical organization.

It seems to me permissible and even desirable for young writers to copy deliberately the style of some author whose work they admire. Take your own subject and write a few pages in the style of some work that appeals to you. It is a way of limbering up your mental muscles and of bringing variety into your own compositions. A study of the ways by which a skillful writer achieves his effects can be enlightening as you develop your own skills. There is no surer way of discovering how he reached his goals than by trying to imitate him. But a little of that goes a long way. Your aim is to achieve your own mode of expression.

Painters frequently follow many schools as they grow. A retrospective exhibition of Picasso's work shows that he tried many styles—there is his classical period, his blue period, his cubistic period. But even his classical period was adapted to his own mood; the same was true when he limited himself to a blue palette. Any artist—whether painter or writer—who remains a copier all his life probably hasn't anything of his own to say.

So school yourself in the practical skills. Learn to research and interview, to write dialogue and anecdotes, to write vivid descriptions of people, places and things, to select what is relevant and to omit what is irrelevant, and finally to build a logical structure. Keep your ear attuned to cadence, your eyes open, your mind aware of what is going on. Revise for clarity and to find precise words, and believe in what you say. Then your style will be inherent in your writing, and that is where it belongs. It is never just an ornament to be tacked on.

Changing times and changing styles

As time passes and as people are faced with new conditions and new problems, sensitive writers and other artists become aware of it and there comes a change in the manner of expression.

There was such a change when I came to New York in the twenties. It was a time of revolt. The First World War was over and young people all over our country were questioning old manners and standards. In Chicago, Carl Sandburg and Edgar Lee Masters and Sherwood Anderson were celebrating a new era. Ellen Glasgow was taking a critical look at the romantic Old South. Sinclair Lewis was pointing out the dullness of the Middle West. Little theaters were showing Eugene O'Neill. Little magazines of protest were springing up. In painting, Boardman Robinson and his fellows of the Ashcan School were exhibiting pictures of the seamy side of life.

Someone gave me a ticket to Carnegie Hall and I heard Stravinsky's *The Firebird* for the first time. I remember my own excitement; I knew little music, but I kept saying to myself, "This is for me. This speaks to my generation." And Hemingway's staccato phrases and his stripped-to-the-bone sentences were exactly right for the time. It was the mood of our youth and oncoming writers got into the swing.

That was a dramatic revolution. But in every generation there are ground swells the writer will watch for. Today we live with another youthful revolution: with rebellion in the colleges, with sit-ins and teach-ins and freedom marches, disdain for old sexual standards and a zeal to help the underprivileged. Again the young writers find a voice for their opinions in the small experimental magazines, in novels and in little theaters. As the years go by, some of these young writers may fizzle out; some, like their forebears of the twenties, may prove to have written classics.

Already some of the ferment is making its way into even our popular journals. In any case these angry young people are part of our time and, whether you scorn them or join them, I suggest that you, at least, make yourself aware of them. Read samples of such literary magazines as *Partisan Review, Commentary,* the *Paris Review,* some of the college magazines and some of the offbeat novels. If you do not have an experimental theater in your community read an occasional play by the American Albee, the French Anouilh, the German Brecht. Many of them are writing in an idiom different from that to which we are accustomed, but their style is their own way of expressing the ideas of the moment.

Another phenomenon today's writer should take notice of is the flowering of cultural centers across the country from Duluth to Los Angeles to Miami to Washington to New York's Lincoln Center, and to many stops along the way. The innumerable symphony orchestras, the crowded art museums and the enormous sales of paperback books, many of them classics, are all evidence of the more literate readers the writer reaches today. All this is reflected in the magazines. From the four-page pamphlet to the heavy slick-paper magazine, almost all our periodicals are well-written and cover a wide range of subjects.

This does not mean that you should address your literate

reader in polysyllabic words. On the contrary, follow Schopenhauer's advice to "use common words to say uncommon things." Cultivate an easy conversational style as if you were talking to your reader across the page. Alan Pryce-Jones reviewing Lord David Cecil's book on Max Beerbohm said, "He writes with charm and sense using the English language as a friend rather than a master." No writer could ask for a higher appraisal of his style.

ℵ 18

PRACTICAL QUESTIONS—AND ANSWERS

What does a literary agent do? What will he do for me? How do I find one? What does he charge?

An agent is a business representative. He knows what most of the important editors of magazines, book publishers, and TV programs are looking for and offers your manuscript for sale to whichever ones he feels would be interested in your material, *if he believes it is publishable.* If he finds a market for your manuscript, he arranges the terms (gets you the highest price and most prestigious publication he can), collects the money, deducts his commission and forwards the proceeds to you. He guards you from bad contracts, helps you keep your copyright straight, and sells your secondary and foreign rights.

To interest an agent, it is well first to write him a query letter describing your work. Many agents today insist that a writer have had published by his own efforts three articles or stories in established magazines before they accept him as a client.

If an agent accepts you as a client, he will often make general suggestions for improving your work; he will suggest subjects, follow up on details, and save you valuable time for your creative work. He can give you encouragement when you need it. But he does not teach you to write, and he does not have time for detailed criticism of your manuscripts.

Not all writers, even well-known ones, have agents. Some prefer to work directly with the editor. But many writers are not good business people; they become confused in their dealings. In that case, an agent can save the author many headaches, and often the agent's commission is more than covered by the better prices he secures, and the additional income he gets from the sales of subsidiary rights, etc.

How do I find an agent? The Authors Guild of America, 234 West 44th Street, New York, will send you a list of reputable agencies.

Without an agent, how do I get published? As a novice writer, send your own articles, or query letters, to the magazines for which you think they are suitable. I suggest that you begin by submitting to some of the hundreds of small magazines scattered throughout the country—to trade papers, to the specialized magazines that treat of your subject, to local newspapers and Sunday supplements, etc. Their payment rates are low, but it is important for you to see your work in print. For lists of publications and their rates see the writer's working library, below.

What does an agent charge? He takes ten per cent commission on sales in the United States and up to twenty per cent on sales in foreign countries. He charges the author for copyright fees and manuscript recopying fees when done at the author's request.

What is the meaning of the term, "first serial rights"?
When a magazine buys first serial rights or first publication rights, it buys the right to publish only once in its own publication. In that case the rights to publication in other magazines, books, movies, radio, television, and foreign rights remain with the author.

What are the advantages of writing for the trade, specialty and little magazines?
As more attainable markets, they are often good places to start. Their specialty may be one that is congenial to you, and often their editors are more willing to work with an up-and-coming author than are the over-burdened editors of the magazine giants.

The mere fact that you have been published will raise your status in any editor's eyes. If, when you write a query letter offering an article on some new synthetic, for instance, you say that you have been a contributor to a magazine on plastics or a related subject, the editor will presume that you know your facts. A contributor to religious publications may arouse more interest when he submits an inspirational idea to a general magazine.

What is a "query letter"? Why should I write it? And how?
A query letter is one you write to an editor telling him of an idea you have for an article, describing it briefly (often

in outline), giving your qualifications for writing on your subject, and asking him if he is interested.

Such a letter will reach the proper editor long before a manuscript would. Numerous unsolicited manuscripts arrive at any publication every day. They are usually read first by readers, who weed out and return the ones that are obviously unsuitable. Those which show promise are passed on to a higher editor who does a further weeding. Finally, the cream of the crop reaches the editor in charge of articles. That editor probably spends his office hours on current administrative and editorial problems and takes home a bulging briefcase for reading at night. By the time he has decided for or against the manuscript, sometimes a week or more will have elapsed.

A query letter, on the other hand, usually reaches the proper editor promptly; its very briefness gives it preference over the longer, completed piece, and a decision can be arrived at without much loss of time. Even then the editor may want to consult other editors on its fitness. If the idea is turned down, the writer can immediately try it out on another publication, and he is saved weeks of suspense.

If the idea appeals to the editor, then the writer may be encouraged to go ahead and develop the piece, or he may be asked to come in to talk it over, or to send in the manuscript. With the way paved for it, the manuscript will usually be read promptly.

If, after the go-ahead, your article is still in the works, your interviewing will go more smoothly, for you can say that such-and-such a publication is interested, and you can go to your final writing with more confidence.

Many magazines insist on a query letter from prospective writers, unless the writer is a regular contributor; even then, they may ask for one.

In preparing your letter, you can often prove to yourself whether or not you have a story. If not, you can turn to another subject.

The query letter, then, is one of the most important jobs a writer faces. To make it a good letter you must prove to the editor that you have material for a piece and that you can write in a professional and acceptable style. Here is a pattern for such a letter:

1. Start off with an opening paragraph to whet the editor's appetite.

2. Then you might go on in so many words, "I'd like to write an article about this," and tell him what your qualifications are for handling your subject.

3. Follow with some of the points you will include.

4. Give at least one anecdote, worked out in detail, or the lead, if you have it, or a couple of paragraphs that will show your style of writing.

5. Finish with a good paragraph, telling him why you think his readers will be interested.

6. Keep your letter to approximately 500 words. Do not tell everything you will include, otherwise, when he receives the complete article, the editor may feel that he has read it all before and forget that it had come originally from you.

Do not write it in the same manner as your actual article. Try to describe it as if you were talking to the editor.

Here is a sample query letter which illustrates its elements:

Mr. John Smith
Articles Editor
Hobson's Magazine
Chicago, Ill.

Dear Mr. Smith:

I am engaged in research for the Blank Foundation on today's unusual opportunities for volunteer workers in many fields. I have become so surprised and fascinated by what I have discovered that I should like to write a timely article on the subject for your magazine.

I majored in sociology and literature in college and before my marriage I was on the staff of *Home* magazine. Since my children have been in school I have served as a volunteer in hospitals, schools and museums in the six states to which my husband's work called us.

The statistics are formidable. There are in our country 0000 thousand institutions that depend on volunteers, over 2000 in New York City alone. There are 000 million citizens who are now doing volunteer work and millions of others are needed. Our growing poverty program is multiplying the demand.

I do not propose a statistical piece. That has been done. My theme is what volunteer work means to the volunteer. I have checked *The Readers' Guide* and find little on that angle.

I propose to lead off with the story of a young woman— drawing on my own experience—her children in school, who is bored with household routine, and follow her ups and downs as she tries to find a niche for her talents. Then continue with stories of a variety of people, rich and poor, teen-agers, middle agers and oldsters who are finding satis- faction in this use of their idle hours.

I was holding forth recently to an executive who stopped

me with, "Keep an eye out for me, will you? I'm up for retirement next year and I dread it. I'm an authority on cor-
porate budgets. Anything there?" I suggested an agency
whose finances were at sixes and sevens. He offered his
services, started working in his spare time, can hardly wait
for his birthday.

Ex-teachers enlist in the Head Start program, a musician
is teaching teenagers to play the guitar, even the harmonica.

TV commentators use their trained voices to read for
records for the blind, young businessmen and career girls
give some evenings and Saturday. All are finding new interests and feeling important.

I have dozens of anecdotes. A young woman, who had
been assigned to spending an afternoon a week with an in-
corrigible 10-year-old in an orphanage, was about to give up
in despair when he said one day, "Could I call you Mom?
You are the only one that belongs to me."

There are amusing incidents, too. Some charities are so-
cially popular and have long waiting lists. The director of
volunteers at one of these is something of a Tartar. "Don't
put *us* on any list," she warned. "I turn them away every
day. I'm not taking any cranky dame just to keep her out
of her daughter-in-law's hair." Yet a great city hospital could
use a thousand more volunteers.

A Negro janitor has taken on six fatherless lads in his
neighborhood, is keeping them in high school and off the
streets. A Puerto Rican woman has formed a mothers' club
to help children. All the religious groups—Catholic Charities, Protestant Federation, Jewish Council, Friends' Service—are recruiting. Many have training programs for volunteers.

I think all your readers, of every age, creed, color and sex,
will be interested. The piece won't be dull or overly senti-
mental; my facts will be accurate.

If you are interested, please tell me what length and emphasis you prefer.

Sincerely,

This letter has an informative lead, gives the writer's qualifications, her theme, the importance of her subject and its timeliness. She includes two anecdotes and human interest details. The diverse people she cites and her mention of the religions involved, indicate a wide reader interest. She writes in a conversational manner, which promises an easy-to-read style. The letter is a little long, but she has a complex subject.

Here is a shorter letter similar to one which brought an immediate expression of interest from the editor. The resulting article was published in the New York Metropolitan section of a large national magazine:

Mr. John Brown, Articles Editor
The National Magazine
120 Blank Street
New York, N.Y.

Dear Mr. Brown:

I should like to write a short article for *The National Magazine*—approximately 2500 words—which I am now calling, "New Yorkers are Repossessing Their Parks."

Our parks have earned the reputation for being danger spots not only with our own citizens, but with people across the country and from abroad. Plane passengers bound for New York, for instance, have been warned never to go alone into Central Park after dusk.

But within the last year, under the stimulus of our new Parks Commissioner, many parks have been restored to the people. A Sunday walk across Central Park a year ago showed a few adults on benches lining the main arteries reading papers, children in fenced-in playgrounds and a scattering of daring souls taking short walks with a wary eye out for the police call boxes. But acres of pleasant and inviting green and the side lanes were unoccupied.

Today, since only the cross-town conduits are open on Sunday to motor traffic until mid-afternoon, there are thousands of bicyclists of all ages pedaling happily along. In the open spaces kites are flying, groups are playing kick ball, toss ball, baseball, football and hockey, boys and girls are seated on the grass or strolling hand-in-hand—people from all walks of life are out for sun and air and pleasure. On weekdays, school boys and girls are out for sports.

While Central Park is our most dramatic example, plans are afoot for similar uses not only for our other large parks, but for the hundreds of tiny bits of green that dot any sizable map of the city.

I will interview the Parks Commissioner on his plans, the police department on safety precautions and people who are finding new pleasure in their city.

I will go briefly into the free entertainment available: the Shakespeare and ballet theaters, the concerts, the children's entertainment and story hours, the seasonal festivals. Also the green spots near our housing projects and schools and the plazas around such buildings as the Time-Life complex.

I think of this as an interesting subject for your New York Metropolitan section. Most of my writing has been for New York papers and Sunday editions, so I know the city well, and I assure you the article will be enlivened with quotes, incidents and human interest.

If you are interested, I will continue my research and hope to have the manuscript in your hands within a month.

Sincerely,

If there is some new development in your own region or an interesting feature that is unique to your section of the country, such a descriptive article might be of interest to the Sunday magazine section of your local paper or to a travel magazine or to the section of a general national publication which goes to your area.

Single-space your letter. (Manuscripts must be double-spaced.) Leave wide margins on which an editor may make notes. And break it into short paragraphs for easy reading. Be sure it is correct in spelling, grammar and punctuation—this is your introduction to the editor. Have it shipshape.

Address your letter to an editor by name; not to The Editor. If you do, it may go through as many hands as a manuscript. Look on the masthead of the magazine for his name. If there is an articles editor or feature editor, address it to him. If there is an editor listed whose title indicates that he is in charge of subjects similar to yours, send your letter to him. If the magazine has a small staff, address your letter to the editor or managing editor by name.

If you have photographs or know where to get them, you might mention that. A sentence such as, "I have photographs," or, "I can direct your photographer to subjects for photographs," will usually take care of that.

Before you write your query letter, make sure you have material for an article. Many writers in their first excitement over a new-found idea rush to the typewriter to ask an editor if he is interested. Wait a minute or a day or a week. Go first to the library and look through *The Readers' Guide* to learn whether the subject has been covered within the last few years. If it has not, then stop in the periodicals room and leaf through current magazines to see whether a similar article is already in circulation. Ideas are contagious. Whatever started your own train of thought may also have occurred to another writer who may have beaten you to it.

If you are writing a personal experience piece, you can stop your preliminary research there. If you are writing on a subject on which you are an authority, unless you have kept posted on what is being published, look further.

If your subject is a profile or based on something you are not thoroughly informed about, return to the library to learn whether there are enough facts available to expand your skimpy knowledge. Look through *The New York Times Index* to find whether your subject has been in the news over the last five or ten years. If your library does not have a file of the *Times,* ask the librarian what other news sources are available. News accounts may give some human interest incidents to add to your letter. They may also mention persons connected with your subject. Learn if you can reach them for an interview.

If your search has shown that enough information is available, *then* you may write your query. I suggest that beginners rough out for themselves a draft of the article, indicating for themselves the gaps they will later fill in. The query will be more convincing.

A query written without this preliminary research is likely to be too vague to convince an editor. Even if your own enthusiasm has brought a go-ahead, you may find too little to make a telling piece. Then you can confess that the article didn't pan out, or send in a flimsy piece that will come back in the next mail. In either case, you have lost face.

If you receive a favorable reply or an expression of interest, return to the library for thorough research and set out to interview the people who have known the subject of your profile or have personal knowledge of the event or thing you are describing. Your preliminary research was merely to assure yourself that you had the makings of an article.

How much time should you spend on such a letter? As much as necessary—your sale depends on it. Some writers rewrite five times.

If you find yourself frozen at the typewriter after you've written "Dear Mr. Smith," at the top of a page, tear out the sheet and start over. Think of someone you know who would be interested in your subject and write an informal letter to that person. It might go, "Dear Aunt Mamie, I came across the most amazing incident the other day," or, "Dear Jim, Did you know that. . . ." and tell her or him your story. Get in as much as you like; it will be too long, but you'll have it down. Cut out your first extravagant statement and begin to organize. Decide on which anecdote you'll keep. Do another draft, or a third or a fourth. Let it rest over night and allow your subconscious to take over. Go at it again when you are fresh next day. You'll be able to spot inconsequential items and needless words and phrases and can edit it for style. First thing you know, you'll have an interesting, informative letter.

Do keep a carbon of your letter. The editor may express an interest, but suggest changes and not return the original. Or he may reject it, and you can revamp the original for a different publication.

Send in only one idea at a time, even if you have a dozen others. You can't write more than one good letter at a time. And a great mishmash of ideas in one envelope is the sign of an amateur. If the editor invites you in for an interview and you find that your first idea is getting no-where, then offer other suggestions; or if he writes that he would like other ideas from you, you can reply with two or at most three other subjects, very briefly described, saying you'll be glad to expand any that appeal to him. Each subject should be on a separate page.

Do be enthusiastic, but don't make extravagant claims. If you write, "This is the most exciting event that has oc-curred in the United States in this century," your follow-up may be viewed with disbelief.

Caution: Do not insert in your query letter a sentence similar to the following: "I should be deeply grateful and encouraged if you would do me the favor of reading my manuscript and helping me with your valuable comments and criticisms." The editor is not a teacher of writing. If he feels your article idea has merit, he may offer comments. Such requests, which often appear in letters from begin-ners, are impositions on a busy person and come only from rank amateurs.

What about seasonal material?

You will save yourself time and postage, if you query the publication first to learn whether it is interested in your subject and point of view. The editor may have on hand another piece on the same subject, or he may not be in the mood for yours at that time.

Don't forget that there is a lag of from two to six months between the time an article is accepted and its appearance on the newsstands. Except for the weeklies, five months is par for the large-circulation magazines. Even the smaller publications work two or three months in advance. After the manuscript is received, it must be edited, copied for art department, printer and files; illustrations must be devised, artists or photographers commissioned, art work delivered and plates engraved, page layouts made, type set and corrected; then to the presses and finally the finished copies mailed so that copies reach California and New York simultaneously on the publication date.

A hard-pressed woman editor I know mourns, "It may be Fourth of July for some folks, but it's Christmas for me." By all means send in any seasonal articles early.

What do I do while I wait for a long-coming answer?

Once you have a query or a manuscript in the mail, go to work on another. Don't sit around watching for the mailman. You should have several queries or manuscripts making the rounds at one time.

Does one ever send out a completed manuscript instead of a query?

If you are a beginner and have difficulty in explaining the treatment you have in mind or your style of writing within a reasonably short query, it is advisable to send the manuscript and take your chances with the manuscript readers. If the merit of your piece takes it to the appropriate editor, he can base his decision not only on your subject matter, but on your ability to organize and on your style. If he likes any of your skills, he may make a personal reply.

In any case it is always well to submit the manuscript

of a humorous piece, which depends largely on treatment and style as well as subject.

What is meant by "regional sections" of magazines?

Many national magazines today publish what are known as regional editions. There may be the northeastern edition, the southeastern edition, etc. Some journals have as many as 25 regional editions. The main body of these publications is the same for the whole nation, but, in addition, there may be included a section in which the articles are selected for the special interests of readers in different parts of the country. For instance, an article on growing tropical plants would be included only in the editions which are circulated in the deep South and would not be included in editions going to other climates.

The *Ladies' Home Journal* usually lists the articles in its regional editions on the contents page. Most other publications do not. You will usually find the regional sections toward the end of the magazine and you can identify them by a different numbering of the pages. For instance, after page 102, you might find an insert especially for your area with pages numbered 102a, 102b, etc. At the end of that section, the regular page numbers would resume—103, 104, etc. Other journals start a new sequence of numbers, such as R1, R2, R3, for the regional sections and at the conclusion resume with 103, 104, etc. An easy way to find these sections is to look toward the end for page numbers which are accompanied by an identifying letter.

These sections are of interest to the writer: if you have an idea for an article that concerns some event or interest peculiar to your part of the country, you may find a place for it in the section for your region. The usual practice is to address your query or manuscript to the national office of the magazine and state that it would be of special interest to readers in your region.

Can you suggest what books I should have for a working library?

1. A good dictionary. I like *The American College Dictionary,* but also look at *Webster's New World Dictionary, The Random House Dictionary of the English Language,* and others. There is also *The Penguin Dictionary of English* (800 pages in paperback).

2. *A Dictionary of Modern English Usage* by H. W. Fowler, new edition, Oxford University Press, or *A Dictionary of American-English Usage,* based on the above, revision by M. Nicholson, Signet paperback. Look also at *Modern American Usage* by Wilson Follett, Hill and Wang.

3. *Roget's International Thesaurus.* For synonyms, I like the Thomas Y. Crowell edition. There are also various paperback versions.

4. *The World Almanac* or the *Information Please Almanac* in paperback, published annually, for statistics and important facts.

OTHER USEFUL BOOKS

1. *Writing and Selling Magazine Articles* by Omer Henry, The Writer, Inc.

2. *The Elements of Style* by William Strunk, Jr., and E. B. White, Macmillan paperbacks.

3. *Say It with Words* by Charles W. Ferguson, Alfred A. Knopf. Also good for style.

4. *The Style Manual* and its *Word Division* supplement, U.S. Government Printing Office, for printing usage.

5. *The Careful Writer* by Theodore M. Bernstein, Atheneum.

6. An up-to-date atlas.

FOR MARKET LISTS

1. *The Writer's Handbook,* edited by A. S. Burack, The Writer, Inc. I find this invaluable not only for its complete lists of all publications, indexed for all classifications from the large general magazines to the little ones, and with rates of payment, but also for its helpful articles by well-known writers.

2. *The Literary Market Place,* R. R. Bowker & Co.

MAGAZINES FOR WRITERS

1. *The Writer,* The Writer, Inc., 8 Arlington Street, Boston, Mass. 02116.

2. *Writer's Digest,* Writer's Digest, 22 East 12th Street, Cincinnati, Ohio 45210.

The Writer is the stand-by for most of my students and also for myself. Both the above magazines contain helpful articles, special monthly market lists, notices of prize contests, of writers' conferences, and lists of new books relating to our profession.

When do I enclose a stamped, return-addressed envelope?

When you are submitting an article, always enclose an envelope of the proper size and affix the proper amount of postage. If you are a beginner, and unknown to the editor, enclose a stamped return envelope with your query letter.

When an editor returns an article he has expressed an interest in and asks me to rewrite, what do I do, especially if I think my own version is best?

First console yourself. It happens to the best of writers.

As an editor I frequently asked authors to rewrite. I had come to the article fresh and often saw where it could be strengthened or made more concise or where information was lacking.

As a writer, my first impulse is to disagree with the editor. I have put in weeks of work and have fallen in love with my own structure and style. But when I have recovered from my first disappointment, and reread my piece with the editor's letter beside me, and then tackled it again, I have always found that the editor was right. When the article was finally accepted and published, I have been grateful for his suggestions. In one case, an editor's request meant rewriting almost the whole piece from a different slant. At other times, it has meant writing a new lead, arranging my topics in a different order, inserting more facts, more or fewer anecdotes, or better ones. So my advice is to accept the editor's judgment.

If you sincerely believe that his point of view is wrong, or you find you can't reshape your material to his specifications, then state your own case to him, and if you can't agree, ask his permission to submit the piece elsewhere.

If I have an article accepted and published in a magazine, and think that "The Reader's Digest" would also be

*interested in it, should I wait until their editors find it, or
can I send in tear sheets to the "Digest" and ask if they
would like it?*

If the first magazine bought only the first serial rights,
there is no reason why you should not call it to the attention of the *Digest.*

Are editors really interested in new writers?

They are indeed, and, when a promising writer comes his
way, an editor will often help the author develop his skills,
work with the writer through three or four drafts of a
possible article, and often make the final corrections and
revisions himself.

A repeated lament in editorial offices is: "Whenever a
staff member comes up with a good article idea we are
forced to give the assignment to one of our regulars. Oh, for
a competent and dependable new writer!" There is mor-
tality among the regulars, too; they may grow old, become
stale or retire. Newcomers are both welcome and necessary
to the survival of the publications.

Be persistent. When an article or query comes back,
don't throw in the sponge. Look at your submission and
try to discover why it was turned down. Perhaps your subject missed the boat. Is it one that would interest the
readers of that publication or any great number of people?
Were you writing for yourself or for your reader? Keep
that reader in the forefront of your mind. Did you have
enough material? Was it poorly written or sloppily presented? Too many articles are.

Compare your piece with published pieces of a similar
kind. What are their good qualities? Don't take a sour-

grapes attitude and tell yourself that your piece is as good or better than some you read. Any published piece has some element the editor liked. Try to find what it is.

And do remember that editors are human. Some have phobias about certain subjects. (One successful editor I knew would never take a piece about a disabled child. Why I never knew. Others have other dislikes.) Or he may not have been in the mood for your piece. Or he may have similar articles on hand or in the works. Or he may have had a bad day when your brain child arrived.

If your own critical appraisal tells you that you still have a good piece, try it on another publication or several. But be sure each time your manuscript or query goes out it looks fresh. A query may need complete retyping; a manuscript may require no more than a retyping of the first few or the last few pages. Never submit either a query or a manuscript to more than one magazine at a time, and wait for the reply before trying it elsewhere.

When you have a letter from an editor telling why your idea is not right for his needs, reread your offering again from his point of view.

Don't be too discouraged over your rejections. Even some established authors count themselves lucky to have three acceptances out of every ten submissions.

Never forget that yours is a craft that thrives on practice, and that times change. So keep yourself alive to the time in which you live.